INTRODUCING
ISSUES WITH
OPPOSING
VIEWPOINTS®

WITHDRAWN

Organic Food and Farming

Lauri S. Friedman, *Book Editor*

GREENHAVEN PRESS
A part of Gale, Cengage Learning

GALE
CENGAGE Learning™

Detroit • New York • San Francisco • New Haven, Conn • Waterville, Maine • London

GALE
CENGAGE Learning™

Christine Nasso, *Publisher*
Elizabeth Des Chenes, *Managing Editor*

© 2010 Greenhaven Press, a part of Gale, Cengage Learning

For more information, contact:
Greenhaven Press
27500 Drake Rd.
Farmington Hills, MI 48331-3535
Or you can visit our Internet site at gale.cengage.com

For product information and technology assistance, contact us at

Gale Customer Support, 1-800-877-4253
For permission to use material from this text or product, submit all requests online at www.cengage.com/permissions

Further permissions questions can be e-mailed to permissionrequest@cengage.com

Articles in Greenhaven Press anthologies are often edited for length to meet page requirements. In addition, original titles of these works are changed to clearly present the main thesis and to explicitly indicate the author's opinion. Every effort is made to ensure that Greenhaven Press accurately reflects the original intent of the authors. Every effort has been made to trace the owners of copyrighted material.

Cover image copyright zing, 2009. Used under license from Shutterstock.com.

LIBRARY OF CONGRESS CATALOGING-IN-PUBLICATION DATA

Organic food and farming / Lauri S. Friedman, book editor.
     p. cm. -- (Introducing issues with opposing viewpoints)
  Includes bibliographical references and index.
  ISBN 978-0-7377-4483-5 (hardcover)
  1. Natural foods--Study and teaching (Secondary) 2. Organic farming--Study and teaching (Secondary) I. Friedman, Lauri S. II. Series: Introducing issues with opposing viewpoints.
  TX369.O65 2009
  641.3'02--dc22
                                                                          2009036912

Printed in the United States of America
1 2 3 4 5 6 7 13 12 11 10 09

Contents

Chapter 3: What Is the Future of Organic Food?

Foreword

I ndulging in a wide spectrum of ideas, beliefs, and perspectives is a critical cornerstone of democracy. After all, it is often debates over differences of opinion, such as whether to legalize abortion, how to treat prisoners, or when to enact the death penalty, that shape our society and drive it forward. Such diversity of thought is frequently regarded as the hallmark of a healthy and civilized culture. As the Reverend Clifford Schutjer of the First Congregational Church in Mansfield, Ohio, declared in a 2001 sermon, "Surrounding oneself with only like-minded people, restricting what we listen to or read only to what we find agreeable is irresponsible. Refusing to entertain doubts once we make up our minds is a subtle but deadly form of arrogance." With this advice in mind, Introducing Issues with Opposing Viewpoints books aim to open readers' minds to the critically divergent views that comprise our world's most important debates.

Introducing Issues with Opposing Viewpoints simplifies for students the enormous and often overwhelming mass of material now available via print and electronic media. Collected in every volume is an array of opinions that captures the essence of a particular controversy or topic. Introducing Issues with Opposing Viewpoints books embody the spirit of nineteenth-century journalist Charles A. Dana's axiom: "Fight for your opinions, but do not believe that they contain the whole truth, or the only truth." Absorbing such contrasting opinions teaches students to analyze the strength of an argument and compare it to its opposition. From this process readers can inform and strengthen their own opinions, or be exposed to new information that will change their minds. Introducing Issues with Opposing Viewpoints is a mosaic of different voices. The authors are statesmen, pundits, academics, journalists, corporations, and ordinary people who have felt compelled to share their experiences and ideas in a public forum. Their words have been collected from newspapers, journals, books, speeches, interviews, and the Internet, the fastest growing body of opinionated material in the world.

Introducing Issues with Opposing Viewpoints shares many of the well-known features of its critically acclaimed parent series, Opposing Viewpoints. The articles are presented in a pro/con format, allowing readers to absorb divergent perspectives side by side. Active reading questions preface each viewpoint, requiring the student to approach the material thoughtfully and carefully. Useful charts, graphs, and cartoons supplement each article. A thorough introduction provides readers with crucial background on an issue. An annotated bibliography points the reader toward articles, books, and Web sites that contain additional information on the topic. An appendix of organizations to contact contains a wide variety of charities, nonprofit organizations, political groups, and private enterprises that each hold a position on the issue at hand. Finally, a comprehensive index allows readers to locate content quickly and efficiently.

Introducing Issues with Opposing Viewpoints is also significantly different from Opposing Viewpoints. As the series title implies, its presentation will help introduce students to the concept of opposing viewpoints and learn to use this material to aid in critical writing and debate. The series' four-color, accessible format makes the books attractive and inviting to readers of all levels. In addition, each viewpoint has been carefully edited to maximize a reader's understanding of the content. Short but thorough viewpoints capture the essence of an argument. A substantial, thought-provoking essay question placed at the end of each viewpoint asks the student to further investigate the issues raised in the viewpoint, compare and contrast two authors' arguments, or consider how one might go about forming an opinion on the topic at hand. Each viewpoint contains sidebars that include at-a-glance information and handy statistics. A Facts About section located in the back of the book further supplies students with relevant facts and figures.

Following in the tradition of the Opposing Viewpoints series, Greenhaven Press continues to provide readers with invaluable exposure to the controversial issues that shape our world. As John Stuart Mill once wrote: "The only way in which a human being can make some approach to knowing the whole of a subject is by hearing what can be said about it by persons of every variety of opinion and studying all modes in which it can be looked at by every character of mind. No wise man ever acquired his wisdom in any mode but this." It is to this principle that Introducing Issues with Opposing Viewpoints books are dedicated.

Introduction

Organic food has entered the mainstream culture, and it is seemingly everywhere. Many of America's largest food manufacturers now offer organic products and feature them on the shelves of the nation's largest grocery stores. Yet, in organic cooperatives—small, locally owned health stores in which the organic foods movement was born—just being "organic" is no longer good enough.

Although mainstream America knows the label "organic" to mean grown without hormones or pesticides, for others involved in the organic movement, the term signifies a lot more. When a product is embraced by what has become known as "small organic" or "nonindustrial organic" consumers, it will also be free of genetic modification. It will have traveled a short distance to reach the store shelf and will preferably have come from a local, independent merchant. It will have been fairly traded and minimally processed. It will have been grown on a *polyculture* farm—a small or medium-size farm that grows a multitude of crops in a way that is most sustainable for the land. It may also be a "cruelty-free" product, which means if any animals were used in the production of the product, they were treated humanely. Given this definition of organic, many co-ops have made decisions to stop carrying organic products they feel are produced in violation of the other ethical principles they think organic foods should reflect.

At the Ocean Beach People's Organic Cooperative Food Market in San Diego, California, simply being produced without pesticides is not enough to get a product on the shelf. For example, the organic brand Tom's of Maine was discontinued at People's when it was bought by Colgate-Palmolive, because that company practices animal testing. Said Amber McHale, the co-op's marketing director, "In keeping with our cruelty-free standards, we could no longer carry that product once it became owned by a company that did not keep with the ethics of the store."[1] Similarly, People's temporarily stopped carrying the popular veggie burger brand Boca Burger when it was bought by the tobacco company Philip Morris. "We certainly were not going to create a profit margin for a tobacco company,"[2] said McHale.

In addition, unlike larger grocery store chains that are eager to feature any organic products on their shelves, People's shoppers will

Wal-Mart began carrying organic foods in 2006. Some say there are important differences between the organic food featured at large stores like Wal-Mart and that carried at small, local, organic food cooperatives.

not find any organic products put out by Kraft Foods, Kellogg's, or General Mills. While these products might feature corn or wheat that has been grown without pesticides, the foods are highly processed and the crops are grown on large-scale farms that do not reflect the other values increasingly important to organic shoppers. "Just because they're organic doesn't mean they're sustainably grown, cruelty-free, free of genetic modification, or locally produced," says McHale. "Our mission is to help people live in ways that are chemical-free but also ecologically sustainable—bringing in the Kraft or Kellogg's 'organic' line is not going to fit with that mission because the products themselves don't fit with it."[3]

Indeed, some view the mainstream adoption of organic food as the death of the whole movement because it compromises the integrity of organic values in exchange for high profits and watered-down criteria. Says *San Francisco Chronicle* columnist Mark Morford, "Kellogg's Organic Rice Krispies. It's sort of like saying 'Lockheed Martin Granola Bars' or 'Exxon Bottled Spring Water.'"[4] Morford and other organic purists believe there is more to organic than just holding back a few pesticides during a product's production. "But the vast majority of organic product now flooding the market only gloms on to that aspect (and sometimes, barely even that)," complains Morford. This is why, in his opinion, "Organic is dead. Corporations have officially bought it out, the USDA [U.S. Department of Agriculture] has weakened its definition to near death, Whole Foods has made it chic and popular and profitable. . . . Those compromises mean 'organic' is a shell of its former self." [5] For Morford and others, this demise officially occurred when Wal-Mart—in their view a classic symbol of unethical corporate greed and soullessness—began carrying a line of organic food in 2006.

Yet others disagree that the mainstreaming of organic means something terrible for the industry or for consumers of organic foods. Consider that more than 200 million Americans shop at Wal-Mart each year. Many of these people are attracted to Wal-Mart because of its bargain prices and would otherwise be unable to afford organic food, which can be 20 to 100 percent more expensive than conventionally produced items. It is argued that offering lower-cost organic food in a store frequented by so many Americans can help improve nutrition and health in the United States, both of which have become national priorities.

Say authors Ann Cooper and Kate Adamick: "When Wal-Mart adds low priced organic produce to the shelves of its 3,400 stores across middle and rural America, chemical-free food will instantly be within reach of tens of millions of individuals currently without access to them." [6] Similarly, the authors foresee a day when McDonald's might decide to start serving organic beef burgers—these will feature organically grown lettuce, tomatoes, pickles, and onions, and be served on buns made from organic wheat. Cooper and Adamick think the availability of chemical-free fast food is something to celebrate and encourage, even if the process needs to be tweaked and perfected.

Whether organic food's foray into the mainstream marks the death of the movement or an exciting breakthrough for it is one of the key debates in this emerging topic. In *Introducing Issues with Opposing Viewpoints: Organic Food and Farming*, readers will consider this and other important issues, such as whether organic food is healthier and more nutritious than conventionally grown foods, whether it is environmentally friendly, whether it can reduce world hunger and global warming, and whether it is a fad that will soon be replaced by another food craze Americans are so famous for embracing. The wealth of information and perspectives provided in the viewpoints will help students form their own opinions about organic food and whether they think it is worth eating.

Notes

1. Amber McHale, interview by author, May 12, 2009.

2. McHale, interview.

3. McHale, interview.

4. Mark Morford, "The Sad Death Of 'Organic': How Weird and Depressing Is It Now That Kellogg's and Wal-Mart Are Hawking 'Natural' Foods?" *San Francisco Chronicle*, October 13, 2006. www .sfgate.com/cgi-bin/article.cgi?f=/gate/archive/2006/10/13/ notes101306.DTL&nl=fix.

5. Morford, "The Sad Death Of 'Organic.'"

6. Ann Cooper and Kate Adamick, "An Organic Foods Dilemma: They're Mass-Produced by Agribiz but Better than Eating Poisons," *San Francisco Chronicle*, August 6, 2006. www.sfgate.com/cgi-bin/article .cgi?f=/c/a/2006/08/06/ING9HKAN4G1.DTL&type=printable.

Chapter 1

Is Organic Food Healthier than Commercially Grown Food?

Labeling foods as organic has become increasingly popular, yet it is debated whether organic foods are significantly healthier than their conventional counterparts.

Viewpoint

1

Organic Food Is More Nutritious than Commercially Grown Food

"The more often we can eat food grown without pesticides, the fewer pesticides we'll consume."

Deborah Rich

In the following viewpoint Deborah Rich argues that organically grown produce is more nutritious than conventionally grown produce. She cites several studies that show that organic food contains more nutrients and minerals and is higher in cancer-preventing antioxidants and flavonoids. Conventionally grown food, on the other hand, has been shown to have significantly fewer nutrients and to contain traces of chemicals and poisons from the fertilizers and pesticides that are used to grow such crops. Rich concludes that organic food is more nutritious than conventional food, and she believes the government should do more to promote its consumption.

Rich writes stories about organic food and other environmental issues for the *San Francisco Chronicle*.

Deborah Rich, "Not All Apples Are Created Equal: Scientists Say Organic Foods Are More Nutritious—Are Government Officials Listening?" *Earth Island Journal,* vol. 23, Spring 2008, pp. 26–30. Copyright © 2008 Earth Island Institute. Reproduced by permission.

Over the past decade, scientists have begun conducting sophisticated comparisons of foods grown in organic and conventional farming systems. They're finding that not all apples (or tomatoes, kiwis, or milk) are equal, especially when it comes to nutrient and pesticide levels. How farmers grow their crops affects, sometimes dramatically, not only how nutritious food is, but also how safe it is to eat. It may well be that a federal food policy that fails to acknowledge the connection between what happens on the farm and the healthfulness of foods is enough to make a nation sick.

The Effect of Fertilizers and Pesticides

In the late 1990s, researcher Anne-Marie Mayer looked at data gathered by the British government from the 1930s to the 1980s on the mineral contents of 20 raw fruits and vegetables. She found that levels of calcium, magnesium, copper, and sodium in vegetables, and of magnesium, iron, copper, and potassium in fruit had dropped significantly.

The 50-year period of Mayer's study coincides with the post World War II escalation of synthetic nitrogen and pesticide use on farms. These agri-chemicals allowed farmers to bypass the methods of maintaining soil fertility by replenishing soil organic matter with cover crops, manure, and compost, and of controlling pests with crop rotation and inter-cropping. Reliance on chemical fertilizers and pesticides became a defining characteristic of conventional farming, while farmers who eschewed the use of agri-chemicals came to be considered organic.

In 2004, Donald R. Davis, a research associate with the BioChemical Institute at the University of Texas at Austin, published a similar analysis of data collected by the USDA [United States Department of Agriculture] in 1950 and again in 1999 on the levels of 13 nutrients in more than 40 food crops. Davis found that while seven nutrients showed no significant changes, protein declined by six percent; phosphorous, iron, and calcium declined between nine percent and 16 percent; ascorbic acid (a precursor of Vitamin C) declined 15 percent; and riboflavin declined 38 percent. Breeding for characteristics like yield, rapid growth, and storage life at the expense of taste and quality were likely contributing to the decline, Davis hypothesized. The "dilution effect," whereby fertilization practices cause harvest weight and dry matter to increase more rapidly than nutrient accumulation can occur, probably also played a role, David suggested.

Organic Food Contains More Minerals and Nutrients

Meanwhile, researchers at the Rodale Institute in Pennsylvania were seeing a trade-off between use of synthetic fertilizers and food nutrient values in the Institute's Farming System Trial.

"We looked at the major and minor nutrients of oat leaves and seeds, grown after 22 years of differentiation under conventional and organic systems," says Paul Hepperly, research and training manager at the Institute. "We found a direct correlation between the increase of organic matter and the amount of individual minerals in the oat leaves and seeds. The increase in minerals ranged from about seven percent for potassium, up to 74 percent for boron. On average, it was between 20 and 25 percent for all the elements we looked at, and we looked at nitrogen, phosphorous, potassium, calcium, magnesium, sulfur, iron, manganese, copper, boron, and zinc. The production practices used on these oats was completely the same the year they were planted—the plots varied only by the legacy of what had happened to the soil as a result of the previous farming practices. This showed how dramatic the soil change had been and its effect on the nutrient content of the plant. We've done these tests not only on oats but also on wheat, corn, soybeans, tomatoes, peppers, and carrots, and we consistently find that the organic heritage improves soil and improves the mineral content of the food products."

Probably due in part to a fertilizer effect, and partly because the use of chemical pesticides dampens the mobilization of a plant's own

University of California, Davis, researchers found that organic tomatoes had much higher levels of the healthy antioxidant compounds quercetin and kaempferol than conventionally grown tomatoes.

defenses, conventionally grown whole foods also often have lower levels of antioxidants and other beneficial phytochemicals than the same foods grown organically.

Charles Benbrook, chief scientist at the Organic Center and former executive director of the Board on Agriculture of the National Academy of Sciences, maintains a database of all the studies published since 1980 that compare the nutrient levels of organic and conventional foods. His analysis of food comparison studies shows that, on average, conventionally grown fruits and vegetables have 30 percent fewer antioxidants than their organically grown counterparts. This makes enough of a difference, says Benbrook, that "consumption of organic produce will increase average daily antioxidant intake by about as much as an additional serving of most fruits and vegetables." . . .

Organic Food Protects and Nourishes

At the University of California at Davis, researchers compared organic and conventional tomatoes. They found that 10-year mean levels of quercetin [an antioxidant] were 79 percent higher in organic tomatoes than in conventional tomatoes, and levels of kaempferol were 97 percent higher. Quercetin and kaempferol are flavonoids, which epidemiological studies suggest offer protection from cardiovascular disease, cancer, and other age-related diseases.

Organic Food Is Worth the Cost

A 2007 Harris poll found that a significant percentage of Americans say organic food is worth its high price, believing that organically grown fruits and vegetables are more nutritious than commercially grown food.

"Which of the following is closer to your opinion?"

Base: All Adults

36%
Organic food is much better for you and, even though it usually costs more, the extra expense is worth it to have better food.

36%
Not sure

29%
Organic food is a waste of money and it is no better for you than conventional foods available in the supermarkets.

A study led by Lukas Rist, head of research at the Paracelsus Hospital in Switzerland, demonstrated how farm practices affect health even several levels up the food chain. Rist analyzed milk samples from 312 breastfeeding mothers. He found that mothers consuming at least 90 percent of their dairy and meat from organic sources have 36 percent higher levels of rumenic acid in their breast milk than mothers eating conventional dairy and meat. Rumenic acid is one of a group of compounds that nutritional research suggests have anti-carcinogenic, anti-diabetic, and immune-modulating effects, and that favorably influence body fat composition. . . .

Pesticides for Breakfast

The toxicity of many of the chemical pesticides used by conventional farmers is of little dispute. Indeed, the [government decides how much pesticide humans can tolerate by] identifying a level of exposure that is acutely toxic to lab animals, then working backwards to identify an exposure level that the EPA [Environmental Protection Agency] feels poses an acceptable threat to human and environmental health.

As our understanding of the body's biochemistry advances, however, EPA-sanctioned levels of pesticide exposure are becoming harder to swallow. . . .

A glance at the data gathered for the USDA Pesticide Data Program reveals that even at breakfast we consume several servings of pesticides. In 2005, 88 percent of apples, 92 percent of milk samples, 52 percent of orange juice samples, 67 percent of wheat samples, and 75 percent of water samples were contaminated with pesticides ranging from herbicides to post-harvest fungicides. None of these pesticides we eat for breakfast gets a clean bill of health. The EPA lists some as probable carcinogens, and others as affecting reproductive and nervous systems.

Exactly how each of us tolerates daily low doses of pesticides will vary according to our genetic heritage, the other industrial toxins we're exposed to, our health, and our age. The very youngest and oldest of us will probably suffer the most damage from pesticide exposure. "At particular moments of development, the immune and neurological systems of infants are profoundly vulnerable to exposure to chemicals," says Benbrook at the Organic Center. "And in the case of the elderly, their livers don't work as well at detoxifying chemicals as they did in the middle part of their lives."

For Better Health, Choose Organic

Logically, the more often we can eat food grown without pesticides, the fewer pesticides we'll consume. . . .

Daily doses of pesticides are particularly unappetizing given the existence of a highly productive model of farming that doesn't need these toxic chemicals. "If you could give me a magic wand and I could make any changes that I want, it would have the EPA researching, developing, and helping farmers implement sustainable agricultural processes so they don't need pesticides," [Center for Environmental Health research director Caroline] Cox says. "There are better ways to manage pests. Organic is a great example that it can be done."

EVALUATING THE AUTHOR'S ARGUMENTS:

To make her argument that organic food is more nutritious than conventionally grown food, Deborah Rich cites several studies. Make a list of all the studies she cites and what their findings are. Which study do you think most helps to support her argument? Why?

Organic Food Is Not More Nutritious than Commercially Grown Food

Rob Johnston

"Organic farmers boast that their animals are not routinely treated with antibiotics . . . but, as a result, organic animals suffer more diseases."

Organic food has no additional health benefits, Rob Johnston argues in the following viewpoint. He explains that organic farmers use pesticides that are even harder on the environment than those used in conventional farming—but in the end, eating traces of pesticides does not threaten one's health, he claims. Furthermore, he says that organic food is actually unhealthier than conventional food—it has been found to contain higher levels of parasites and bacteria and no higher levels of nutrients and minerals. He concludes that the benefits of organic food have been hyped by the organic food industry in an attempt to make money.

Rob Johnston is a doctor and science writer.

AS YOU READ, CONSIDER THE FOLLOWING QUESTIONS:
1. If pesticides were dangerous to people, what group of people does Johnston say would have high cancer rates?
2. What percentage of organic chickens does Johnston say are infected with parasites?
3. What, according to Johnston, caused a study to find that organic tomatoes contain higher levels of the nutrient group flavonoids?

The great organic myths: Why organic foods are an indulgence the world can't afford.

They're not healthier or better for the environment – and they're packed with pesticides. In an age of climate change and shortages, these foods are an indulgence the world can't afford, argues environmental expert Rob Johnston.

Myth One: Organic Farming Is Good for the Environment

The study of Life Cycle Assessments (LCAs) for the UK, sponsored by the Department for Environment, Food and Rural Affairs, should concern anyone who buys organic. It shows that milk and dairy production is a major source of greenhouse gas emissions (GHGs). A litre of organic milk requires 80 per cent more land than conventional milk to produce, has 20 per cent greater global warming potential, releases 60 per cent more nutrients to water sources, and contributes 70 per cent more to acid rain.

Also, organically reared cows burp twice as much methane as conventionally reared cattle—and methane is 20 times more powerful a greenhouse gas than CO_2. Meat and poultry are the largest agricultural contributors to GHG emissions. LCA assessment counts the energy used to manufacture pesticide for growing cattle feed, but still shows that a kilo of organic beef releases 12 per cent more GHGs, causes twice as much nutrient pollution and more acid rain.

Life Cycle Assessment (LCA) relates food production to: energy required to manufacture artificial fertilisers and pesticides; fossil fuel burnt by farm equipment; nutrient pollution caused by nitrate and phosphate run-off into water courses; release of gases that cause acid rain; and the area of land farmed. A similar review by the University of Hohenheim, Germany, in 2000 reached the same conclusions (Hohenheim is a proponent of organic farming and quoted by the Soil Association).

Myth Two: Organic Farming Is More Sustainable

Organic potatoes use less energy in terms of fertiliser production, but need more fossil fuel for ploughing. A hectare of conventionally farmed land produces 2.5 times more potatoes than an organic one.

Heated greenhouse tomatoes in Britain use up to 100 times more energy than those grown in fields in Africa. Organic yield

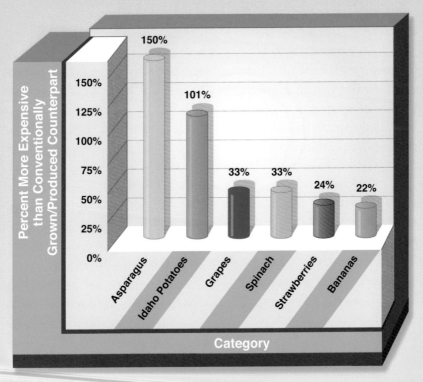

Paying Top Dollar for Organic Foods

Consumers can pay more than twice as much for certain organic fruits and vegetables, according to a *Consumer Reports* study that compared price averages of organic and conventional produce in the New York area. Those who believe organic food is no healthier think it is a waste of money.

Taken from: *Consumer Reports*, 2005.

is 75 percent of conventional tomato crops but takes twice the energy—so the climate consequences of home-grown organic tomatoes exceed those of Kenyan imports.

Defra estimates organic tomato production in the UK releases almost three times the nutrient pollution and uses 25 per cent more water per kg of fruit than normal production. However, a kilogram of wheat takes 1,700 joules (J) of energy to produce, against 2,500J for the same amount of conventional wheat, although nutrient pollution is three times higher for organic.

Myth Three: Organic Farming Doesn't Use Pesticides

Food scares are always good news for the organic food industry. The Soil Association and other organic farming trade groups say conventional food must be unhealthy because farmers use pesticides. Actually, organic farmers also use pesticides. The difference is that "organic" pesticides are so dangerous that they have been "grandfathered" with current regulations and do not have to pass stringent modern safety tests.

For example, organic farmers can treat fungal diseases with copper solutions. Unlike modern, biodegradable, pesticides copper stays toxic in the soil for ever. The organic insecticide rotenone (in derris) is highly neurotoxic to humans—exposure can cause Parkinson's disease. But none of these "natural" chemicals is a reason not to buy organic food; nor are the man-made chemicals used in conventional farming.

Myth Four: Pesticide Levels in Conventional Food Are Dangerous

The proponents of organic food—particularly celebrities, such as Gwyneth Paltrow, who have jumped on the organic bandwagon—say there is a "cocktail effect" of pesticides. Some point to an "epidemic

Organic chickens roam freely around their barn. The author says that organically grown chickens are contaminated with more parasites and salmonella than conventionally raised ones.

of cancer". In fact, there is no epidemic of cancer. When age-standardised, cancer rates are falling dramatically and have been doing so for 50 years.

If there is a "cocktail effect" it would first show up in farmers, but they have among the lowest cancer rates of any group. Carcinogenic effects of pesticides could show up as stomach cancer, but stomach cancer rates have fallen faster than any other. Sixty years ago, all Britain's food was organic; we lived only until our early sixties, malnutrition and food poisoning were rife. Now, modern agriculture (including the careful use of well-tested chemicals) makes food cheap and safe and we live into our eighties.

Myth Five: Organic Food Is Healthier

To quote Hohenheim University: "No clear conclusions about the quality of organic food can be reached using the results of present literature and research results." What research there is does not support the claims made for organic food.

Large studies in Holland, Denmark and Austria found the food-poisoning bacterium Campylobacter in 100 per cent of organic chicken flocks but only a third of conventional flocks; equal rates of contamination with Salmonella (despite many organic flocks being vaccinated against it); and 72 per cent of organic chickens infected with parasites.

This high level of infection among organic chickens could cross-contaminate non-organic chickens processed on the same production lines. Organic farmers boast that their animals are not routinely treated with antibiotics or (for example) worming medicines. But, as a result, organic animals suffer more diseases. In 2006 an Austrian and Dutch study found that a quarter of organic pigs had pneumonia against 4 per cent of conventionally raised pigs; their piglets died twice as often.

Disease is the major reason why organic animals are only half the weight of conventionally reared animals—so organic farming is not necessarily a boon to animal welfare.

Myth Six: Organic Food Contains More Nutrients

The Soil Association points to a few small studies that demonstrate slightly higher concentrations of some nutrients in organic produce—flavonoids in organic tomatoes and omega-3 fatty acids in organic milk, for example.

The easiest way to increase the concentration of nutrients in food is to leave it in an airing cupboard for a few days. Dehydrated foods contain much higher concentrations of carbohydrates and nutrients than whole foods. But, just as in humans, dehydration is often a sign of disease.

The study that found higher flavonoid levels in organic tomatoes revealed them to be the result of stress from lack of nitrogen – the plants stopped making flesh and made defensive chemicals (such as flavonoids) instead.

Myth Seven: The Demand for Organic Food Is Booming

Less than 1 per cent of the food sold in Britain is organic, but you would never guess it from the media. The Soil Association positions itself as a charity that promotes good farming practices. Modestly, on its website, it claims: ". . . in many ways the Soil Association can claim to be the first organisation to promote and practice sustainable development." But the Soil Association is also, in effect, a trade group—and very successful lobbying organisation.

Every year, news outlets report the Soil Association's annual claim of a big increase in the size of the organic market. For 2006 (the latest available figures) it boasted sales of £1.937bn.

Mintel (a retail consultantcy hired by the Soil Association) estimated only £1.5bn in organic food sales for 2006. The more reliable TNS Worldpanel, (tracking actual purchases) found just £1bn of organics sold—from a total food sector of £104bn. Sixty years ago all our food was organic so demand has actually gone down by 99 per cent. Despite the "boom" in organics, the amount of land being farmed organically has been decreasing since its height in 2003. Although the area of land being converted to organic usage is scheduled to rise, more farmers are going back to conventional farming.

The Soil Association invariably claims that anyone who questions the value of organic farming works for chemical manufacturers and agribusiness or is in league with some shady right-wing US free-market lobby group. Which is ironic, considering that a number of British fascists were involved in the founding of the Soil Association and its journal was edited by one of Oswald Mosley's blackshirts until the late 1960s.

All Britain's food is safer than ever before. In a serious age, we should talk about the future seriously and not use food scares and misinformation as a tactic to increase sales.

EVALUATING THE AUTHOR'S ARGUMENTS:

Rob Johnston is a doctor. Does knowing his background encourage you to believe him when he argues that organic foods are no more nutritious than conventionally grown foods? Why or why not? Explain your reasoning.

Viewpoint 3

Organic Food Has Significant Health Benefits

André Leu

"The facts show that organic food has significant health benefits because it has negligible chemical residues and pathogens and higher nutritional values."

In the following viewpoint André Leu explains why he believes organic food has significant health benefits. He claims that organic food is richer in the vitamins, minerals, and nutrients that keep people healthy, younger-looking, and cancer-free. For example, he says organic produce is rich in antioxidants, which fight cancer, and is also high in compounds that protect the immune system. Furthermore, organic food contains significantly lower levels of pesticides than conventionally grown food, and Leu claims such pesticides have been linked to a higher incidence of breast, uterine, prostate, and other cancers. For all of these reasons, Leu concludes that eating organic can help people live healthier, longer lives.

Leu owns a certified organic farm in North Queensland, Australia. He is the chair of the Organic Federation of Australia.

André Leu, "The Benefits of Organic Food," Organic Federation of Australia, December 4, 2003. Reproduced by permission.

AS YOU READ, CONSIDER THE FOLLOWING QUESTIONS:
1. What is "salicylic acid," and how much more of it does Leu say
   organic vegetable soups contain?
2. What was the conclusion of a UN Food and Agriculture
   Organization report, according to Leu?
3. What three substances does Leu say are prohibited in the production of organic livestock?

Many people purchase organic food because they believe it is healthier than conventionally grown food. The organic industry is constantly told that there is no evidence to support these claims. [In fact,] organic food is substantially healthier than conventional food. Research published in a 2001 study showed that the current fruit and vegetables in the United States have about half the vitamin content of their counterparts in 1963. The study was based on a comparison of published USDA figures.

Higher Levels of Cancer-Fighting Nutrients and Protective Compounds

A scientific study published in the *Journal of Applied Nutrition* in 1993 clearly showed that organic food is more nutritious than conventional food. Organically and conventionally grown apples, potatoes, pears, wheat and sweet corn were purchased over two years in the western suburbs of Chicago, and then analyzed for mineral content. The organically grown food was on average 63 percent higher in calcium, 73 percent higher in iron, 118 percent higher in magnesium, 178 percent higher in molybdenum, 91 percent higher in phosphorus, 125 percent higher in potassium, and 60 percent higher in zinc. In addition, the organic food was on average 29 percent lower in mercury than the conventionally raised food.

A peer-reviewed scientific article published in the February 2003 *Journal of Agricultural and Food Chemistry* stated that organically grown corn, strawberries and marionberries have significantly higher levels of cancer-fighting antioxidants than conventionally grown foods. Some of these compounds, such as flavonoids, are phenolic compounds that have potent antioxidant activities. Many are produced by plants in

A UN Food and Agriculture Organization report concluded that the superior management practices used in organic poultry farming reduce the risk of E. coli *infection in animals such as turkeys.*

response to environmental stresses, such as insects or competing plants. They are protective compounds that act as a plant's natural defense and also have protective properties in human and animal health.

The research suggested that pesticides and herbicides disrupt the production of these protective compounds. Good soil nutrition appears to increase the levels of these natural compounds that have anti-cancer, immune-boosting and anti-aging properties. Another peer-reviewed scientific study, published in the *European Journal of Clinical Nutrition*, showed a higher level of protective phytonutrients in organic food. Dr. John Paterson and a team from the University of Strathclyde, U.K., found that organic vegetable soups contain almost six times as much salicylic acid as non-organic vegetable soups. Salicylic acid is produced naturally in plants as a protective compound against stress and disease. It is responsible for the anti-inflammatory action of aspirin, and helps combat hardening of the arteries and bowel cancer.

The average level of salicylic acid in 11 brands of organic vegetable soup on sale in Britain was 117 nanograms per gram, compared with 20 ng/g in 24 types of non-organic soups. The highest concentration of salicylic acid, 1,040 ng/g, was found in an organic carrot and coriander soup, while it was not detectable in four conventional soup brands.

Organic Food Gives People the Nutrients They Need

Two comprehensive studies have been published that compared the differences between organic and conventional foods. Both studies analyzed around 40 previously published studies. One study was conducted in the United Kingdom and the other in the United States, each independently of the other. Both studies came up with similar conclusions that there is overwhelming evidence that organic food is more nutritious than conventional food. One of the authors stated, "On average our research found higher vitamin C, higher mineral levels and higher phytonutrients—plant compounds which can be effective against cancer. There's also less water in organic vegetables, so pound-for-pound you get more carrot for your carrot." It is no coincidence that consumer demand for food supplements has grown as the amount of minerals and vitamins has declined in conventionally farmed food. Many people cannot get the necessary quantity and quality of nutrition from food grown with synthetic chemicals.

Organic Livestock Is Not Contaminated

In the recent past there have been a number of media stories claiming that, because organic foods are grown with manure, they contain higher levels of dangerous pathogens. On investigation, all of these stories were proved to be false, and most of the media presenters apologized publicly for promoting inaccurate and misleading stories. It is a requirement of organic certification systems either that animal manures be composted or that two non-food rotations be grown on a manured site before it can be used for small crops. In fact, a UN Food and Agriculture Organization report concluded that the superior management practices of organic agriculture reduce E. coli [a bacterium] and mycotoxin [a fungus-produced toxin] infections in food: "It can be concluded that organic

> **FAST FACT**
>
> A 2006 study published in a National Institutes of Health journal showed that children who eat a conventional diet have metabolic evidence of pesticide exposure in their urine. However, when they were switched to an organic diet, the signs of exposure disappeared.

farming potentially reduces the risk of E. coli infection. . . . Two studies reported by Woess found that aflatoxin [a toxic, cancer-causing type of mycotoxin] M1 levels in organic milk were lower than in conventional milk. . . . As organically raised livestock are fed greater proportions of hay, grass and silage, there is reduced opportunity for mycotoxin-contaminated feed to lead to mycotoxin-contaminated milk." The report further stated, "Animal feeding practices followed in organic livestock production also lead to a reduction in contamination of food products of animal origin."

The use of antibiotics, antimicrobials, and hormones or other growth promoters is prohibited in organic production. Where animals are treated with veterinary chemicals, they are not allowed to be sold as organic. Similarly, the use of synthetic chemicals as preservatives, colorings, antioxidants, etc., is prohibited in the processing of organic foods. There is an increasing body of concern about these synthetic compounds in the diets of humans and animals used for human food.

Fewer Chemical Residues

Many studies show that most conventionally farmed foods have pesticide and other chemical residues. Repeated tests show that many of these foods can carry a cocktail of synthetic poisons. A growing body of scientific evidence is showing that repeated exposures to cocktails of small amounts of synthetic chemicals produce a range of adverse health effects. A recently published study shows that as little as one-tenth of a part per billion of one commonly used herbicide can damage reproductive systems. In addition, many scientists believe these exposures of minute quantities of agricultural chemicals are very significant for children. A study by the U.S. Centers for Disease Control found a cocktail of many toxic chemicals in the blood and urine of most Americans that they tested. Other studies show that most living organisms carry a cocktail of synthetic/manmade chemicals. Only now are scientists beginning to understand the detrimental effects of minute amounts of these artificial toxins.

Peer-reviewed, published research has demonstrated that many of these types of chemicals are known to disrupt the hormone, nervous and immune systems. The escalating increase of certain types of cancers such as lymphoma, leukemia, breast, uterine and prostate cancers are linked to agricultural and other synthetic chemicals. Similarly, a good body of scientific research also links these chemicals to dramatic increases in autoimmune diseases such as asthma and chronic fatigue syndrome, and non-Hodgkin's lymphoma has gone from being one of the rarest to one of the fastest growing cancers among people exposed to agricultural chemicals.

A detailed scientific analysis of organic fruits and vegetables published in the peer-reviewed journal *Food Additives and Contaminants*

"YOU GET WHAT YOU PAY FOR"

"You Get What You Pay For," cartoon by Andy Singer, PoliticalCartoons.com, July 23, 2005. © 2005 Andy Singer and PoliticalCartoons.com. All rights reserved.

showed that organic foods have significantly less pesticide residues than conventionally grown foods.

Most important, scientific studies are beginning to show that eating organic food results in lower levels of these pervasive chemicals in humans. A study published in the peer reviewed journal *Environmental Health Perspectives* found that children who eat organic foods have lower levels of one class of agricultural pesticides in their bodies. The University of Washington researchers who conducted the study concluded, "The dose estimates suggest that consumption of organic fruits, vegetables, and juice can reduce children's exposure levels from above to below the EPA's current guidelines, thereby shifting exposures from a range of uncertain risk to a range of negligible risk. Consumption of organic produce appears to provide a relatively simple way for parents to reduce their children's exposure to OP [organophosphate] pesticides." . . .

The Health Benefits Are Clear

The FAO states the case very succinctly: "It has been demonstrated that organically produced foods have lower levels of pesticide and veterinary drug residues and, in many cases, lower nitrate contents. Animal feeding practices followed in organic livestock production also lead to a reduction in contamination of food products of animal origin."

The facts show that organic food has significant health benefits because it has negligible chemical residues and pathogens and higher nutritional values when compared to conventionally farmed food.

EVALUATING THE AUTHORS' ARGUMENTS:

Leu argues that even though organic animals are not treated with antimicrobials or other disease-reducing pathogens, they stay free of bacteria and parasites because of the way organic farmers tend to the livestock. How do you think Rob Johnston, the author of the previous viewpoint, would respond to this claim? After considering both authors' claims, with whom do you ultimately agree on the safety of organic meat? Why?

There Is No Evidence That Organic Food Has Significant Health Benefits

"There really is no proof that organic food, which costs about a third more, is better for us than the conventionally grown stuff."

Judy Foreman

In the following viewpoint Judy Foreman reports there is no evidence that organic food has significant health benefits. Although the organic food industry makes a lot of money every year, she says, it remains unclear whether paying more for organic food is actually worth it. Organic food simply means it is grown without pesticides—yet Foreman reports that scientists and doctors are not convinced that eating trace amounts of pesticides is all that harmful. She admits that meat treated with hormones is probably unhealthy but points out that both organic and nonorganic meat comes hormone-free. She concludes that eating a lot of fruit and vegetables, regardless of how they are grown, is more important than eating organic produce.

Foreman is a reporter for the *Boston Globe.*

AS YOU READ, CONSIDER THE FOLLOWING QUESTIONS:
1. Who is George Blackburn, and what risk does he think fruit and vegetables grown with pesticides pose?
2. What kind of cancer does Foreman say has been linked to the consumption of meat treated with hormones?
3. What were the findings of a Danish study published in the *Journal of the Science of Food and Agriculture*, as reported by Foreman?

With the recession breathing down our necks, you may be looking for ways to cut the household budget without seriously compromising family well-being. So here's a suggestion: If you buy organic fruits and veggies, consider going for the less pricey nonorganic produce instead.

No Proof That Organic Is Better

I know, I know, abandoning an organic way of life seems unthinkable in this chemical age. But hold the e-mails and hear me out. There really is no proof that organic food, which costs about a third more, is better for us than the conventionally grown stuff.

Yes, it makes sense, intuitively, that crops grown without pesticides should be better for us. It's appealing, politically, to think that food grown the old-fashioned way, by rotating crops and nurturing the soil naturally, would be superior to food that is mass-produced and chemically-saturated.

Many people feel that way. Sales of organic food and beverages have grown from $1 billion in 1990 to well over $20 billion this year, according to the Organic Trade Association, an industry group.

But the unfortunate truth is that, from a hard-nosed science point of view, it's still unclear how much better, if at all, organic food is for human health.

Understanding What "Organic" Means

"Organic," for the record, means food grown without most conventional pesticides or fertilizers made with synthetic ingredients, according to the US Department of Agriculture's website (usda.gov). To carry the "organic" seal, a product must be certified by a federally accredited agent as having been produced according to federal regulations. Small farmers are exempt.

Prepared food made with organic ingredients also tends to be processed more gently, with fewer chemical additives, said Charles Benbrook, an agricultural economist who is chief scientist at the Organic Center. The nonprofit research group is based in Boulder, Colo., and supported by individuals and the organic food industry.

But the word organic has not been designated as an official "health claim" by the government. Such a designation is used only when there is evidence of significant health benefits—and so far, that evidence is lacking for organic food.

How Dangerous Are Pesticides?

It's clear, however, that conventionally grown food has remnants of pesticides on it. A 2002 study in the journal *Food Additives and*

Differences Between Organic and Conventionally Grown Foods

The kinds of pesticides, fertilizers, and farming techniques are a few of the ways in which conventionally and organically produced foods differ. Experts point out the foods themselves are not different, just the way they are produced.

Conventional Farming	Organic Farming
Apply chemical fertilizers to promote plant growth.	Apply natural fertilizers, such as manure or compost, to feed soil and plants.
Spray insecticides to reduce pests and disease.	Use insects and birds, mating disruption, or traps to reduce pests and disease, or "natural" pesticides like the bacterium Bt (*Bacillus thuringiensis*).
Use chemical herbicides to manage weeds.	Rotate crops, till, hand weed, or mulch to manage weeds.
Give animals antibiotics, growth hormones, and medications to prevent disease and spur growth.	Give animals organic feed and allow them access to the outdoors. Use preventative measures—such as rotational grazing, a balanced diet, and clean housing—to help minimize disease.

Taken from: Center for American Progress, 2008.

Contaminants showed there are more pesticide residues on conventional than organically grown food, even after the food is washed and prepared. There's also clear evidence that pesticides can get into people, a major reason Environmental Protection Agency regulations exist to keep farm workers from entering recently sprayed fields.

A study by Emory University researchers and others published in 2006 in *Environmental Health Perspectives*, a peer-reviewed journal published by the National Institutes of Health, showed that when children are fed a conventional diet, their urine shows metabolic evidence of pesticide exposure, but that when they are switched to an organic diet, those signs of exposure disappear.

All of which raises the question: How much harm do the pesticides cause?

A number of studies suggest that, at high doses, organophosphate chemicals used in pesticides can cause acute poisoning, and even at somewhat lower doses may impair nervous system development in children and animals. But at the amounts allowed by the government in the American food supply? That's where nutritionists and environmental scientists seem to part company.

The term "organic" simply means food grown without most conventional fertilizers and pesticides that are made from synthetic ingredients.

ORGANIC

Very Low Health Risk

"We don't have any good proof that there is any harm from fruits and vegetables grown with the pesticides currently used," said Dr. George Blackburn, a nutritionist at Beth Israel Deaconess Medical Center and associate director of the Division of Nutrition at Harvard Medical School. The real issue is to get people to eat more fruits and vegetables, whether they're grown conventionally or organically, he added.

"Keeping herbicide and pesticide levels as low as possible does make sense, although there is no clear evidence that these increase health risks at the levels consumed currently in the US, "said Dr. Walter Willett, chairman of the department of nutrition at the Harvard School of Public Health.

What is of growing concern, he said, is the meat industry's increasing use of growth hormones in animals. Those hormones may be linked to breast cancer in women, he said. (The "organic" label on beef means, among other things, that it was raised without antibiotics and hormones. Some nonorganic beef is also raised without hormones or antibiotics, as noted on its label.)

Even if we don't yet have all the evidence that organic veggies and fruit might be desirable, Benbrook of the Organic Center said it's time to change the old notion that "there's nothing wrong with a little pesticide for breakfast." Over the last two years, he said, "nearly every issue of Environmental Health Perspectives has had at least one new research report" on how pesticides can harm a child's neurological growth, particularly on "brain architecture, learning ability and markers for ADHD [attention deficit hyperactivity disorder]." While this falls short of incontrovertible "proof" that properly washed conventional produce can harm us, it does raise red flags, environmentalists say.

Mixed Results on the Value of Organic

Weighing the value of organic foods also means looking at nutrition, not just the danger of pesticides—and there is also disagreement over whether organic food supplies more nutrients.

Researchers at the University of California, Davis, did a 10-year study in which a particular strain of tomatoes was grown with pesticides on conventional soil right next to the same strain grown on soil that was certified organic. All plants were subject to the same weather, irrigation, and harvesting conditions.

The conclusion? Organic tomatoes had more vitamin C and health-promoting antioxidants, specifically flavonoids called quercitin and kaemperfol—although researchers noted that year-to-year nutrient content can vary in both conventional and organic plants.

Other studies have also shown nutritional advantages for organic food, according to the Organic Center, which reviewed 97 studies on comparative nutrition. Benbrook, the center's chief scientist, says that although conventionally grown food tends to have more protein, organic food is about 25 percent higher in vitamin C and other antioxidants.

Yet a recent Danish study published in the *Journal of the Science of Food and Agriculture* showed no vitamins and minerals advantage to organic food.

So, what to eat? I side with the nutritionists who urge us to eat more fruits and veggies, regardless of how they're grown.

EVALUATING THE AUTHOR'S ARGUMENTS:

Judy Foreman says that since there is no overwhelming proof that organic food is healthier than conventional food, people should not spend their money on it. In your opinion, is money the only issue here? Can you think of any other reason why it may or may not be a good idea to buy organic food if it is not actually offering any health benefit? Use what you know so far on the topic to answer the question.

Organic Food Is Safer than Conventional Food

Andrew Schneider

"It is appropriate to assume that if we—human beings—are exposed to (this class of) pesticides . . . there are going to be some health concerns down the road."

In the following viewpoint Andrew Schneider reports that eating organic food is safer because it contains fewer chemicals than conventionally grown food. He describes the results of a yearlong study that followed children who ate both organic and nonorganic food. The children who ate nonorganic food had much higher levels of poisonous chemicals from pesticides in their systems than the children who ate organic food. Schneider warns that these chemicals could be connected to birth defects; behavioral, learning, and neurological problems; and other health issues. He concludes the government should tighten its standards of what level of pesticides is deemed safe for consumption.

Schneider is a senior correspondent for the *Post-Intelligencer*, a daily newspaper serving the Seattle area.

Andrew Schneider, "Harmful Pesticides Found in Everyday Food Products," *Intelligencer* (Seattle), January 30, 2008. Reproduced by permission of the author.

AS YOU READ, CONSIDER THE FOLLOWING QUESTIONS:
  1. What is chlorpyrifos, and what does the author say is its effect on the body?
  2. What is the Food Quality Protection Act, as described by the author?
  3. Who is Chuck Benbrook, and what is his opinion of the Environmental Protection Agency's allowable pesticide limits in food?

Government promises to rid the nation's food supply of brain-damaging pesticides aren't doing the job, according to the results of a yearlong study that carefully monitored the diets of a group of local children.

The peer-reviewed study found that the urine and saliva of children eating a variety of conventional foods from area groceries contained biological markers of organophosphates, the family of pesticides spawned by the creation of nerve gas agents in World War II.

When the same children ate organic fruits, vegetables and juices, signs of pesticides were not found.

"The transformation is extremely rapid," said Chensheng Lu, the principal author of the study published online in the current issue of *Environmental Health Perspectives.*

"Once you switch from conventional food to organic, the pesticides (malathion and chlorpyrifos) that we can measure in the urine disappears. The level returns immediately when you go back to the conventional diets," said Lu, a professor at Emory University's School of Public Health and a leading authority on pesticides and children.

Within eight to 36 hours of the children switching to organic food, the pesticides were no longer detected in the testing.

The subjects for his testing were 21 children, ages 3 to 11, from two elementary schools and a Montessori preschool on Mercer Island.

The community has double the median national income, but the wealth of Mercer Island made no difference in the outcome, he said.

"We are confident that if we did the same study in poor communities, we would get the same results," he said. The study is being repeated in Georgia.

The study has not yet linked the pesticide levels to specific foods, but other studies have shown peaches, apples, sweet bell peppers, nectarines, strawberries and cherries are among those that most frequently have detectable levels of pesticides.

Measuring the Harm

Lu is quick to point out that there is no certainty that the pesticides measured in this group of children would cause any adverse health outcomes. However, he added that a recent animal study demonstrated that persistent cognitive impairment occurred in rats after chronic dietary exposure to chlorpyrifos.

Death or serious health problems have been documented in thousands of cases in which there were high-level exposures to malathion and chlorpyrifos. But a link between neurological impairments and repeated low-level exposure is far more difficult to determine.

"There's a large underpinning of animal research for organophosphate pesticides, and particularly for chlorpyrifos, that points to bad outcomes in terms of effects on brain development and behavior," Dr. Theodore Slotkin, a professor of pharmacology and cancer biology at Duke University in North Carolina, said in the April 2006 *Environmental Health Perspectives*.

Lu says more research must be done into the harm these pesticides may do to children, even at the low levels found on food.

The author, an Environmental Protection Agency pesticide adviser, says that even low-level spraying of pesticides will cause health problems later in life for people who have been exposed.

Conventional Produce Is Contaminated with Pesticides

A study by the Environmental Working Group analyzed results of nearly 51,000 tests for pesticides on fruits and vegetables conducted by the USDA and the FDA between 2000 and 2005. They found that many of the most commonly eaten fruits and vegetables contain measurable levels of pesticides.

Produce	Percentage of Samples Tested with Detectable Pesticides
Peaches	96.6%
Apples	93.6%
Sweet Bell Peppers	81.5%
Celery	94.1%
Nectarines	97.3%
Strawberries	92.3%
Cherries	91.4%
Lettuce	68.2%
Grapes, Imported	84.2%
Pears	86.2%
Spinach	70.0%
Potatoes	81.0%
Carrots	81.7%
Green Beans	67.6%
Hot Peppers	55.0%
Cucumbers	72.5%
Raspberries	47.9%
Plums	74.0%
Oranges	85.1%
Grapes, Domestic	60.5%
Cauliflower	84.6%
Tangerines	66.7%
Mushrooms	60.2%
Cantaloupe	53.3%
Lemons	55.6%
Honeydew Melon	59.2%
Grapefruit	62.9%
Winter Squash	41.3%
Tomatoes	46.9%
Sweet Potatoes	58.4%
Watermelons	38.5%
Blueberries	27.5%
Papaya	23.5%
Eggplant	23.4%
Broccoli	28.1%

Taken from: *Environmental Health Perspectives*, 2008.

"In animal and a few human studies, we know chlorpyrifos inhibits an enzyme that transmits a signal in the brain so the body can function properly. Unfortunately, that's all we know."

Not many chemicals, including pharmaceutical products, were designed specifically to kill mammals, which was the genesis of organophosphates.

"It is appropriate to assume that if we—human beings—are exposed to (this class of) pesticides, even though it's a low-level exposure on a daily basis, there are going to be some health concerns down the road," said Lu, who is on the Environmental Protection Agency's pesticide advisory panel.

The EPA says it eliminated the use of organophosphates on many crops and imposed numerous restrictions on the remaining organophosphate pesticide uses.

Congressional concern that children were being harmed by excessive exposure to pesticides led to the unanimous passage of the Food Quality Protection Act. At its heart was a requirement that by 2006, the EPA complete a comprehensive reassessment of the 9,721 pesticides permitted for use and determine the safe level of pesticide residues permitted for all food products.

> **FAST FACT**
>
> A 2002 study published in the journal *Food Additives and Contaminants* showed there were more pesticide residues on conventional than organically grown food, even after the food was washed and prepared.

"As a result, the amount of these pesticides used on kids' foods (has undergone) a 57 percent reduction," said Jonathan Shradar, the EPA's spokesman.

But that's not nearly enough to prevent birth defects and neurological problems, said Chuck Benbrook, chief scientist of the Organic Center, a nationwide, nonprofit, food research organization.

"The pesticide limits that EPA permits are far, far too high to say they're safe. And, the reduction that EPA cites in the U.S. has been accompanied by a steady increase in pesticide-contaminated imported foods, which are capturing a growing share of the market," he said.

Yet the EPA continues to insist that "dietary exposures from eating food crops treated with chlorpyrifos are below the level of concern for the entire U.S. population, including infants and children."

That statement is "not supported by science," Benbrook said.

"Given the almost daily reminders that children are suffering from an array of behavioral, learning, neurological problems, doesn't it make sense to eliminate exposures to chemicals known to trigger such outcomes like chlorpyrifos?" he asked.

What to Do

While the gut reaction of some parents might be to limit the consumption of fresh produce or switch completely to organic food, Lu cautions not to make the wrong decision.

"It is vital for children to consume significantly more fresh fruits and vegetables than is commonly the case today," he says, citing such problems as juvenile diabetes and obesity.

"Nor is our purpose to promote the consumption of organic food, although our data clearly demonstrate that food grown organically contains far less pesticide residues."

Lu says an all-organic diet is not necessary. He has two sons, 10 and 13, and he estimates that about 60 percent of his family's diet is organic.

"Consumers," he says, "should be encouraged to buy produce direct from the farmers they know. These need not be just organic farmers, but conventional growers who minimize their use of pesticides."

Understanding how fruits and vegetables grow can help guide the consumer, he says.

For example, organic strawberries probably are worth the money because they are a tender-fleshed fruit grown close to the dirt, so more pesticides are needed to fight insects and bugs from the soil. He adds apples and spinach to his list.

"It may also be money-smart to choose conventionally grown broccoli because it has a web of leaves surrounding the florets, resulting in lower levels of pesticide residue," Lu says.

He is greatly concerned about one finding from the study.

"Overall pesticide (marker) levels in urine samples were even higher in the winter months, suggesting children may have consumed fruits and vegetables that are imported. The government needs to ensure that imported food comply with the standards we impose on domestic produce," he said.

Dangerous Science

Chlorpyrifos, made by Dow Chemical Co., is one of the most widely used organophosphate insecticides in the United States and, many believe, the world.

For years, millions of pounds of the chemical insecticide were used in schools, homes, day care centers and public housing, and studies show that children were often exposed to enormously high doses. Just as the EPA was ready to ban the product, which analysts said would have damaged Dow's overseas sales, the company "voluntarily" removed it from the home market. Yet, with few exceptions, the agricultural uses continued.

The EPA's Web site is a study in contradictions when it comes to chlorpyrifos.

At one section, it "acknowledged the special susceptibility and sensitivity of children to developmental and neurological effects from exposure to chlorpyrifos."

But in another section, the agency reports that infants and children face no risk from eating food crops treated with chlorpyrifos. However, the agency doesn't say how it reached that conclusion. There is no agreement of how much of the neurotoxin is too much.

Benbrook said the EPA has refused orders from Congress to study the cumulative developmental risk to children from low-dose exposures.

"Perhaps we can rest assured that EPA has protected us adults from acute insecticide poisoning risk, but our kids are on their own," Benbrook said.

EVALUATING THE AUTHORS' ARGUMENTS:

To make his argument, Schneider cites sources that say people who eat conventional foods have higher traces of pesticides in their systems. He also says that these levels of pesticides are probably harmful. How do you think Judy Foreman, author of the previous viewpoint, would respond to these claims? Quote at least one of the authors in your answer.

Organic Food Is Not Any Safer than Conventional Food

Kim Severson and Andrew Martin

> *"Organic certification technically has nothing to do with food safety."*

In the following viewpoint Kim Severson and Andrew Martin argue that organic food is not necessarily safer than conventional food. They discuss how the organic industry has become big business, generating millions of dollars per year. As it has grown, the industry has become more reliant on a complicated web of food providers, not all of which practice basic sanitation or follow required health inspections. Organic food simply means it is produced without pesticides—but there is no guarantee that it is necessarily safer or less prone to food-borne illness than conventional foods, they argue. In fact, certain kinds of organic foods may be *more* prone to bacteria and parasites because those producers opt not to use chemicals and practices that prevent such issues.

Severson and Martin are reporters for the *New York Times*.

AS YOU READ, CONSIDER THE FOLLOWING QUESTIONS:
1. By 2002, how do the authors say the organic food movement had changed?
2. How many people do the authors say were sickened and killed in a 2009 salmonella outbreak in peanut products, some of which were organic?
3. What does the word "dysfunctional" mean in the context of the viewpoint?

MOST of the chicken, fruit and vegetables in Ellen Devlin-Sample's kitchen are organic. She thinks those foods taste better than their conventional counterparts. And she hopes they are healthier for her children.

Lately, though, she is not so sure.

The national outbreak of salmonella in products with peanuts has been particularly unsettling for shoppers like her who think organic food is safer.

The plants in Texas and Georgia that were sending out contaminated peanut butter and ground peanut products had something else besides rodent infestation, mold and bird droppings. They also had federal organic certification.

"Why is organic peanut butter better than Jif?" said Ms. Devlin-Sample, a nurse practitioner from Pelham, N.Y. "I have no idea. If we're getting salmonella from peanut butter, all bets are off."

Although the rules governing organic food require health inspections and pest-management plans, organic certification technically has nothing to do with food safety.

"Because there are some increased health benefits with organics, people extrapolate that it's safer in terms of pathogens," said Urvashi Rangan, a senior scientist and policy analyst with Consumers Union, the nonprofit publisher of *Consumer Reports*. "I wouldn't necessarily assume it is safer."

But many people who pay as much as 50 percent more for organic food think it ought to be. The modern organic movement in the United States was started by a handful of counterculture farmers looking to grow food using methods that they believed were better for the land and produced healthier food. It was a culture built on purity and trust that emphasized the relationship between the farmer and the customer.

By 2002, those ideals had been arduously translated into a set of federal organic regulations limiting pesticide use, restricting kinds of animal feed and forbidding dozens of other common agricultural practices.

To determine who would be allowed to use the green and white "certified organic" seal, the Department of Agriculture deputized as official certifiers dozens of organizations, companies and, in some cases, state workers.

These certifiers, then, are paid by the farmers and manufacturers they are inspecting to certify that the standards have been met. Depending on several factors, the fee can be hundreds or thousands of dollars. Manufacturers who buy six or seven organic ingredients to make one product are especially dependent on the web of agents.

If agents do a thorough job, the system can be effective. But sometimes it falls apart.

Texas officials last month fired a state worker who served as a certifier because a plant owned by the Peanut Corporation of America—the company at the center of the salmonella outbreak—was allowed to keep its organic certification although it did not have a state health certificate.

A private certifier took nearly seven months to recommend that the U.S.D.A. revoke the organic certification of the peanut company's Georgia plant, and then did so only after the company was in the thick of a massive food recall. So far, nearly 3,000 products have been recalled, including popular organic items from companies like Clif Bar and Cascadian Farm. Nine people have died and almost 700 have become ill.

FAST FACT

According to the financial advice Web site SmartMoney.com, to feed eight people an organic Thanksgiving meal, a shopper would pay $295.36 more than a nonorganic meal—a premium of $126.35, or 75 percent.

The Peanut Corporation of America had its organic certification revoked by the USDA in the wake of the 2009 peanut butter salmonella outbreak.

The private certifier, the Organic Crop Improvement Association, sent a notice in July to the peanut company saying it was no longer complying with organic standards, said Jeff See, the association's executive director. He would not say why his company wanted to pull the certification.

A second notice was sent in September, but it wasn't until Feb. 4 that the certifier finally told the agriculture department that the company should lose its ability to use the organic label.

Mr. See said the peanut company initially appeared willing to clear up the problems. But he said the company was slow to produce information and then changed the person in charge of the organic certification, further delaying the process.

He said his organization finally decided to recommend suspending the organic certification after salmonella problems at the plant were exposed.

Although certifiers have some discretion in giving organic companies time to fix compliance problems, Barbara C. Robinson, acting director of the agriculture department's National Organic Program, said her agency is investigating the gap between the first notice of noncompliance and the recommendation that the peanut plant surrender its organic certification.

To emphasize that reporting basic health violations is part of an organic inspector's job, Ms. Robinson last week issued a directive to the 96 organizations that perform foreign and domestic organic inspections that they are obligated to look beyond pesticide levels and crop management techniques.

Potential health violations like rats—which were reported by federal inspectors and former workers at the Texas and Georgia plants—must be reported to the proper health and safety agency, the directive said.

"For example, while we do not expect organic inspectors to be able to detect salmonella or other pathogens," Ms. Robinson wrote, "their potential sources should be obvious from such evidence as bird, rodent and other animal feces or other pest infestations."

Even some certifiers say that while their job is not to assure that food is safe, taking account of health inspections will help consumers.

"It's a reassurance that they have another set of eyes, and more eyes is always a good thing," said Jane Baker, director for sales and marketing of California Certified Organic Farmers, a nonprofit certifying organization in Santa Cruz, Calif., and one of the largest and oldest in the country. "But let's not confuse food safety controls with the organic side of things."

Organics has grown from an $11 billion business in the United States in 2001 to one that now generates more than $20 billion in sales, so the stakes for farmers, processors and certifiers can be high. But the agency overseeing the certifying process has long been considered underfunded and understaffed. Critics have called the system dysfunctional.

Arthur Harvey, a Maine blueberry farmer who does organic inspections, said agents have an incentive to approve companies that are paying them.

"Certifiers have a considerable financial interest in keeping their clients going," he said.

Meanwhile, consumers are becoming more skeptical about certification, said Laurie Demeritt, president of the Hartman Group, a market research firm.

Some shoppers want food that was grown locally, harvested from animals that were treated humanely or produced by workers who were paid a fair wage. The organic label doesn't mean any of that.

"They're questioning the social values around organics," Ms. Demeritt said.

The Organic Trade Association, which represents 1,700 organic companies, wants to shore up organic food's image. This week it's beginning a $500,000 Web-based campaign on the benefits of organic food with the slogan: "Organic. It's worth it."

"You may not feel any healthier right away, but you'll definitely feel more smug," cartoon by Mike Baldwin. www.CartoonStock.com. © Mike Baldwin. Reproduction rights obtainable from www.CartoonStock.com.

Supporters of the National Organic Program think additional money in the recent farm bill will help improve its reach.

And great hope is being placed in Kathleen A. Merrigan, director of the agriculture, food and environment program at Tufts University, who was appointed the deputy agriculture secretary last week. Dr. Merrigan helped design the national organic standards, and is seen as a champion of organic farmers and someone who can help clarify and strengthen federal food laws.

Meanwhile, consumers remain perplexed about which food to buy and which labels assure safer and better-tasting food.

Emily Wyckoff, who lives in Buffalo, buys local food and cooks from scratch as much as possible. Although she still buys organic milk and organic peanut butter for her three children, the organic label means less to her these days—especially when it comes to processed food in packages like crackers and cookies.

"I want to care, but you have to draw the line," she said.

But the line stops when it comes to basic food safety.

Recently, a sign near the Peter Pan and Skippy at her local grocery store declared that those brands were safe from peanut contamination. There was no similar sign near her regular organic brand.

"I bought the national brand," she said. "Isn't that funny?"

EVALUATING THE AUTHORS' ARGUMENTS:

Severson and Martin argue that organic food is not necessarily safer than conventionally produced food. How do you think the other authors represented in this chapter would respond to this claim? Write two sentences on how you think each author would respond, and use at least one piece of evidence from each viewpoint.

Chapter 2

Can Organic Farming Improve the World?

An organic farm employee in Switzerland inspects crops. Switzerland has a long tradition of organic farming.

Organic Food Is Environmentally Friendly

Dave Ring

"Organic agriculture is ecologically sustainable and therefore good for the environment."

Dave Ring is the owner of an organic food store in Muncie, Indiana. In the following viewpoint he explores the ways in which organic food is environmentally friendly. One way is that organic food is farmed without the use of pesticides and toxic fertilizers, both of which pollute the soil and water supply and kill organisms that do not threaten crops. Furthermore, organic farming tends to be a local endeavor, which means that local residents are kept employed by the industry and food travels fewer miles to get to their stores. Finally, Ring claims that organic farming promotes socially responsible, ethical employment practices that benefit whole communities. For all of these reasons, he views organic farming as an environmentally friendly practice that should be more widely adopted in the United States.

AS YOU READ, CONSIDER THE FOLLOWING QUESTIONS:

1. What, according to Chelsea Butler, is directly linked to an animal's diet, lifestyle, and health?

2. What does Ring report organic fields are fertilized with? Why is this better than what conventional fields use for fertilizer?
3. In what way can organic farming help minimize social problems, according to Gerry Waite?

W hat is organic food? Why eat organic food? What can organic farming do to help people and the planet?
Luckily we don't have to answer the first question very often anymore. Most people now understand that organic food is simply food that is produced without synthetic chemicals. No pesticides, no chemical fertilizers, and no growth hormones or antibiotics in livestock, and no processing of food with industrial nasties. But do we know the answers to the last two questions? Why should we eat organic food? There can potentially be dozens of answers to this question, but I have basically broken the answers down into five main reasons.

1. It just tastes better.
2. It's better for human health.
3. It's ecologically sustainable and therefore good for the environment.
4. It builds local economies and has a lot of economic impact.
5. It benefits human culture in a number of different ways.

These are some serious claims to make, I know. . . . So, one by one we'll answer these claims with opinions from local experts and we'll see if we can start a community conversation.

Organic Food Is Free of Pesticides and Wax

Chelsea Butler, a local Ivy Tech culinary school instructor, Ball State Dining Supervisor, and finally, a part time chef at The Blue Bottle Coffee Shop, offers up the following opinion that is shared by most modern forward-thinking chefs today. . . .

"Of course organic (food) tastes better. Fresh produce absorbs flavor from the soil. Non organic produce uses pesticides, waxes, and chemical fertilizers to make up for poor farming methods, greatly affecting overall quality and taste. The flavor of animal products (dairy, meat, and eggs) is directly linked to the animal's diet, lifestyle, and health.

Many organic farms rely more than conventional farms do on humans to do jobs that take place on the farm itself. For this reason, supporters say they are good for the economy. "Direct" refers to jobs on the farm; "indirect" refers to jobs related to farm activity; "induced" refers to jobs in the community made possible by the spending of those with direct and indirect farm jobs.

Labor Income per 1,000 Acres

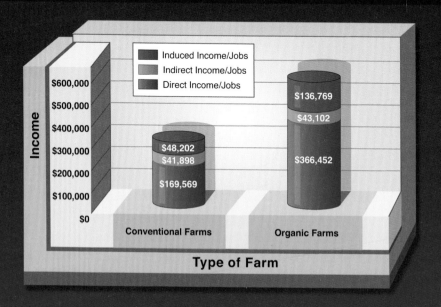

Taken from: Leopold Center for Sustainable Agriculture, March 2007.

Small, organic farms that pay attention to these details will always have a superior taste and quality. There's nothing delicious about growth hormones, disease, and the lack of ethics used in the factory farming industry."

Dr. Michael Williamson is an Oncologist at Medical Consultants in Muncie [Indiana] and is an organic food consumer and advocate. He offers up the following view about one of the effects that eating organic food has on human health. "The benefits of organic foods and products will help ease the burden of detoxification by the liver and other biochemical mechanisms. It's healthier in general for everyone."

Organic Farming Is Ecologically Sustainable

Organic agriculture is ecologically sustainable and therefore good for the environment.

Dr. Hugh Brown is an Associate Professor Emeritus in the Natural Resources and Environmental Management Department at Ball State University. Dr. Brown is a former Chair of the department and was the instructor of the Sustainable Agriculture class at Ball State University. Dr. Brown offers us the following answer on some ways that organic agriculture is better for the environment.

"One key advantage for organic production over industrial agricultural operations is the environmental safety of avoiding pesticide use. Most pesticides do not control the target organism which causes the bulk of the material to affect organisms that we are trying to protect such as beneficial insect predators that help keep pests in balance. The fertilization of fields with organic amendments such as manures and compost provides both essential plant nutrients and a carbon source for soil microorganisms. The favorable structure created by the microbes helps improve the soil's resistance to erosion."

Helping Local Business Thrive

Tom Steiner is a counselor and a business advisor with the Indiana Small Business Development Center. When asked the question about how he thinks the growth of organic agriculture in our area can improve the local economy, he gave us the following answer.

> **FAST FACT**
>
> According to the Rodale Institute, if organic agriculture was practiced on the planet's 3.5 billion farmable acres, it could sequester nearly 40 percent of current CO_2 emissions and help reduce global warming.

"From an economic standpoint, local farmers get a higher share of the consumer's money spent on food. This means that money is recirculated locally and not removed from the community. Because the food is local, there is less transportation time to get the food to market and this means less cost and fresher food for consumers. Probably the biggest impact local organic farming can have on a community is the creation of jobs.

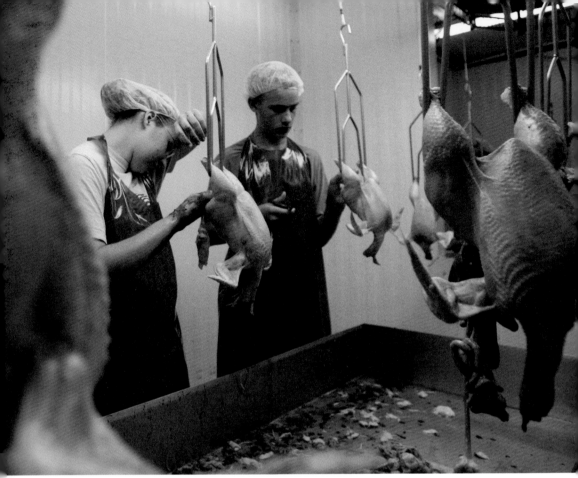

The author says that organic farms—like this one run by a family in Texas—create jobs by relying primarily on human workers rather than large machines.

Organic farming can be more labor intensive, so job creation is part of the process of building a local sustainable food system.

Local organic farming is probably one of the best business models when it comes to building strong middle class independent businesses. These are the types of businesses that help grow and sustain a community.

Organic Farming Benefits Society

In speaking with Ball State University Cultural Anthropology Instructor Gerry Waite, I learned that, in his view, employing more people in rural areas can help to eliminate social problems. Gerry says, "Sustainable organic agriculture is more family oriented and will therefore support more people on the land. Organic farming and sustainable local food systems will increase population density in rural areas. Industrial agriculture employs fewer people and leaves more people behind. Every person you can employ will eliminate another set of social problems in society. If you take care of the local economy, then you can solve many problems. Industrial agriculture is not sustainable in the long run."

EVALUATING THE AUTHOR'S ARGUMENTS:

Dave Ring bases his argument on quotes from several sources in his community. Make a list of the people he quotes, including their credentials and the nature of their comments. Then, analyze his sources—are they credible? Are they well qualified to speak on this subject?

Organic Food Is Not Environmentally Friendly

"Organic farmers are bound to an ideology that . . . gets in the way of practices that are better for the environment and more sustainable for farmers."

Elizabeth Finkel

Organic farming is not always good for the environment, Elizabeth Finkel argues in the following viewpoint. She argues that in trying to avoid chemical use and genetic engineering, organic farming techniques actually take a greater toll on the environment than some conventionally farmed crops. For example, she points out that organic crops use natural pesticides that are not completely environmentally friendly. Furthermore, since these crops are not protected by other types of pesticides, natural pesticides must be sprayed in excess, which threatens soil, groundwater, and life. In addition, Finkel says that organic crops do not produce as much food as conventional crops. Therefore, if more farmers were to switch to organic growing methods, forests would have to be cut down to make room for fields—a practice which is neither environmental nor sustainable. For these and other reasons she concludes that organic farming is not the model environmental practice it is purported to be.

Finkel is a science writer based in Melbourne, Australia. She is the author of *Stem Cells: Controversy on the Frontiers of Science*.

AS YOU READ, CONSIDER THE FOLLOWING QUESTIONS:
1. What is BT, and how does the author say it makes organic crops less environmentally friendly than genetically modified crops?
2. What are two negative effects of the organic pesticides sulphur and rotenone, according to Finkel?
3. What ethical practices are pursued by both organic and nonorganic farmers, according to Finkel?

I love my local organic food store. From the moment I enter, I enjoy the aromas that greet me and the folksy look of the place. But is organic food really any better for me? The perceived wisdom is that it's more 'pure' and 'natural', devoid of disease-causing pesticides; that organic farming "generates healthy soils" and "doesn't poison ecosystems with toxic chemicals". . . . But is this belief in organic food based on faith, or evidence? . . .

Organic Crops Overuse Certain Pesticides
Organic farmers are bound to an ideology that demands they only use natural techniques. In some cases, such purism gets in the way of practices that are better for the environment and more sustainable for farmers. For example, organic farmers will use litres of BT spray (BT is a 'natural' pesticide made by the bacterium *Bacillus thuringiensis*), yet they often demonise the genetically modified (GM) cotton crops that carry an inbuilt supply of BT, and which therefore require less spraying.

However, these GM varieties spare farmers—and the environment—from the risks of pesticide overuse. For instance, according to Richard Roush, the Dean of land and food resources at the University of Melbourne, cotton farmers in India have reduced their use of pesticides and accidental poisonings by 80 per cent since the introduction of genetically modified BT cotton.

Organic Crops Threaten Forests
The ultimate test of sustainability is whether organic farming could feed the planet. Scott Kinnear, president of Australia's Organic

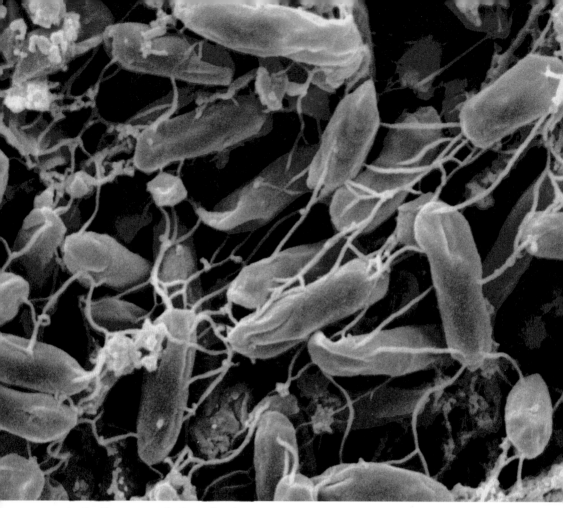

An electron micrograph of Bacillus thuringiensis *shows toxin protein crystals (in purple) that are used in agricultural and forestry pest control.*

Farmers Federation, believes "it is imperative that the world moves over to organic farming as soon as possible".

Yet many agricultural scientists estimate that if the world were to go completely organic, not only would the remaining forests have to be cleared to provide the organic manure needed for farming, the world's current population would likely starve.

Norman Ernest Borlaug, the American plant geneticist who won a Nobel Peace Prize for breeding the high-yield, disease-resistant wheat varieties (triggering agriculture's 'Green Revolution'), is despairing of the organic fad. "This shouldn't even be a debate. Even if you could use all the organic material you have—the animal manures, the human waste, the plant residues—and get them back on the soil, you couldn't feed more than four billion people."

"Natural" Does Not Mean "Harmless"

To get high yields from food crops requires disturbing nature to deliver just what the crops need. First off, crops need fertiliser, which is often nitrogen in the form of nitrate and ammonia, because most plants can't draw nitrogen directly from the atmosphere. (Legumes are a famous exception—their root nodules hold bacteria that turn atmospheric nitrogen into nitrate.) Second, there has to be a way of stopping all the other robust plant and insect species from competing with or consuming your crop.

Non-organic farmers make use of chemicals to achieve these goals. Just prior to World War I, German chemists Fritz Haber and Carl Bosch learned to make ammonia synthetically. Their chemical reaction is still used today to produce more than 450 million tonnes of artificial fertiliser per year, and sustains the agriculture which feeds about 60 per cent of the Earth's population.

Organic farmers source nitrate from manures, gradually broken down by soil organisms. They use only naturally-occurring products to control pests, such as the elements sulphur and copper; pyrethrins and rotenone (both made by plants); BT spray and Spinosad (both made by bacteria). However, these natural pesticides are not harmless. For instance, sulphur irritates the lungs, and rotenone has been shown to cause Parkinson's disease in rats.

> **FAST FACT**
>
> Eighty-five percent of organic food in Canada is imported from great distances. Even vegetables that could be grown locally—such as garlic, potatoes, carrots and apples—are regularly trucked from thousands of miles away.

Certified organic farmers (those accredited by one or more of the six voluntary associations [in Australia], from the Organic Growers of Australia to the National Association for Sustainable Agriculture) also subscribe to a code that includes kinder treatment of animals, a commitment to sustainability and environmental health, fair trade and social equity. But many of these practises are also pursued by 'non-organic' farmers. . . .

Earth's climate changing fast, and the human population heading for nine or 10 billion, we need solutions based on scientific evidence rather than faith and good intentions.

EVALUATING THE AUTHOR'S ARGUMENTS:

Finkel points out that genetically modified crops require less sprayed pesticide because they come with pesticides built into their genetic code. In this sense, she views them as more environmentally friendly than organic crops. What do you think of this argument? Does it improve or weaken your perception of organic food and farming? Explain your reasoning.

Organic Farming Saves Energy

Ed Hamer and Mark Anslow

"Organically grown crops use 25 percent less energy than their chemical cousins."

In the following viewpoint Ed Hamer and Mark Anslow explain several ways in which organic farming saves energy. For one, they claim organic crops use less energy by using natural, recycled, or renewable materials to fertilize crops and power farm equipment. Secondly, organic farming techniques prevent greenhouse gases such as carbon dioxide from entering the atmosphere. Carbon dioxide is among the gases believed to be causing climate change, and thus Hamer and Anslow believe organic farming can, like driving less or switching to renewable energy sources, help prevent global warming. Finally, the authors say that organic food is more likely to come from local sources than is conventional food, and thus saves the energy required to ship food around the globe. For all of these reasons they conclude that organic farming saves energy and is environmentally friendly.

Anslow is a senior reporter for the *Ecologist*; Hamer is a writer whose work has also appeared in the *Ecologist*.

Ed Hamer and Mark Anslow, "10 Reasons Why Organic Can Save the World," *Ecologist,* January 3, 2008. Reproduced by permission.

AS YOU READ, CONSIDER THE FOLLOWING QUESTIONS:
  1. How much less energy do the authors say organic leeks and broccoli use, compared to their conventionally farmed counterparts?
  2. According to Hamer and Anslow, how does organic farming keep carbon dioxide, a greenhouse gas, out of the atmosphere?
  3. How many miles do the authors say the average meal travels in the United Kingdom?

Currently, we use around 10 calories of fossil energy to produce one calorie of food energy. In a fuel-scarce future, which experts think could arrive as early as 2012, such numbers simply won't stack up.

Organic Crops Are "Energy-Lite"

Studies by the [UK] Department for Environment, Food and Rural Affairs (Defra) over the past three years have shown that, on average, organically grown crops use 25 per cent less energy than their chemical cousins. Certain crops achieve even better reductions, including organic leeks (58 per cent less energy) and broccoli (49 per cent less energy). When these savings are combined with stringent energy conservation and local distribution and consumption (such as organic box schemes [companies delivering boxes of organic produce to customers' homes]), energy-use dwindles to a fraction of that needed for an intensive, centralised food system. A study by the University of Surrey shows that food from Tolhurst Organic Produce, a smallholding in Berkshire, which supplies 400 households with vegetable boxes, uses 90 per cent less energy than if non-organic produce had been delivered and bought in a supermarket.

Far from being simply 'energy-lite', however, organic farms have the potential to become self-sufficient in energy—or even to become energy exporters. The 'Dream Farm' model, first proposed by Mauritius-born agroscientist George Chan, sees farms feeding manure and waste from livestock and crops into biodigesters, which convert it into a methane-rich gas to be used for creating heat and electricity. The residue from these biodigesters is a crumbly, nutrient-rich fertilizer, which can be spread on soil to increase crop yields or further digested by algae and used as a fish or animal feed.

Organic Crops Save on Greenhouse Gas Emissions

Despite organic farming's low-energy methods, it is not in reducing demand for power that the techniques stand to make the biggest savings in greenhouse gas emissions.

The production of ammonium nitrate fertiliser, which is indispensable to conventional farming, produces vast quantities of nitrous oxide—a greenhouse gas with a global warming potential some 320 times greater than that of CO_2. In fact, the production of one tonne of ammonium nitrate creates 6.7 tonnes of greenhouse gases (CO_2), and was responsible for around 10 per cent of all industrial greenhouse gas emissions in Europe in 2003.

A farm worker in Argentina starts a biogas engine that runs on methane gas produced from pig manure. Organic farms are environmentally friendly when they recycle waste and save energy.

The techniques used in organic agriculture to enhance soil fertility in turn encourage crops to develop deeper roots, which increase the amount of organic matter in the soil, locking up carbon underground and keeping it out of the atmosphere. The opposite happens in conventional farming: high quantities of artificially supplied nutrients encourage quick growth and shallow roots. A study published in 1995 in the journal *Ecological Applications* found that levels of carbon in the soils of organic farms in California were as much as 28 per cent higher as a result. And research by the Rodale Institute shows that if the US were to convert all its corn and soybean fields to organic methods, the amount of carbon that could be stored in the soil would equal 73 per cent of the country's (would-be) Kyoto targets for CO_2 reduction.[1]

FAST FACT

According to an article in *BioScience Magazine*, organic agriculture can reduce greenhouse gas emissions: Organic crops use 28 to 32 percent fewer energy inputs than conventional systems and do a better job of retaining soil carbon and nitrogen.

Organic farming might also go some way towards salvaging the reputation of the cow, demonised in 2007 as a major source of methane at both ends of its digestive tract. There's no doubt that this is a problem: estimates put global methane emissions from ruminant livestock at around 80 million tonnes a year, equivalent to around two billion tonnes of CO_2, or close to the annual CO_2 output of Russia and the UK combined. But by changing the pasturage on which animals graze to legumes such as clover or birdsfoot trefoil (often grown anyway by organic farmers to improve soil nitrogen content), scientists at the Institute of Grassland and Environmental Research believe that methane emissions could be cut dramatically. Because the leguminous foliage is more digestible, bacteria in the cow's gut are less able to turn the fodder into methane. Cows also seem naturally to prefer eating birdsfoot trefoil to ordinary grass.

1. The Kyoto Protocol is an international agreement that sets targets for participating countries for reducing greenhouse gas emissions. The United States, as of early 2009, had not ratified the protocol.

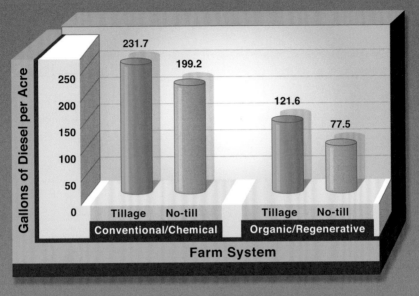

Organic Farming Saves Energy

Organic and regenerative farm systems have been found to require less diesel fuel per acre to plant and raise corn crops.

Gallons of Diesel per Acre

231.7
199.2
121.6
77.5

| Tillage | No-till | Tillage | No-till |

Conventional/Chemical   Organic/Regenerative

Farm System

Taken from: Rodale Institute, 2008.

Saving Water

Agriculture is officially the most thirsty industry on the planet, consuming a staggering 72 per cent of all global freshwater at a time when the UN says 80 per cent of our water supplies are being overexploited.

This hasn't always been the case. Traditionally, agricultural crops were restricted to those areas best suited to their physiology, with drought-tolerant species grown in the tropics and water-demanding crops in temperate regions. Global trade throughout the second half of the last century led to a worldwide production of grains dominated by a handful of high-yielding cereal crops, notably wheat, maize and rice. These thirsty cereals—the 'big three'—now account for more than half of the world's plant-based calories and 85 per cent of total grain production.

Organic agriculture is different. Due to its emphasis on healthy soil structure, organic farming avoids many of the problems associated with compaction, erosion, salinisation and soil degradation, which are prevalent in intensive systems. Organic manures and green mulches are applied even before the crop is sown, leading to a process known as 'mineralisation'—literally the fixing of minerals in the soil. Mineralised organic matter, conspicuously absent from synthetic fertilisers, is one of the essential ingredients required physically and chemically to hold water on the land.

Organic management also uses crop rotations, undersowing and mixed cropping to provide the soil with near-continuous cover. By contrast, conventional farm soils may be left uncovered for extended periods prior to sowing, and again following the harvest, leaving essential organic matter fully exposed to erosion by rain, wind and sunlight. In the US, a 25-year Rodale Institute experiment on climatic extremes found that, due to improved soil structure, organic systems consistently achieve higher yields during periods both of drought and flooding.

Keeping Food Local Saves Energy

The globalisation of our food supply, which gives us Peruvian apples in June and Spanish lettuces in February, has seen our food reduced to a commodity in an increasingly volatile global marketplace. Although year-round availability makes for good marketing in the eyes of the biggest retailers, the costs to the environment are immense.

Friends of the Earth estimates that the average meal in the UK travels 1,000 miles from plot to plate. In 2005, Defra released a comprehensive report on food miles in the UK, which valued the direct environmental, social and economic costs of food transport in Britain at £9 billion each year. In addition, food transport accounted for more than 30 billion vehicle kilometres, 25 per cent of all HGV [heavy goods vehicles—large trucks] journeys and 19 million tonnes of carbon dioxide emissions in 2002 alone.

The organic movement was born out of a commitment to provide local food for local people, and so it is logical that organic marketing encourages localisation through veg boxes, farm shops and stalls. Between 2005 and 2006, organic sales made through direct marketing outlets such as these increased by 53 per cent, from £95 to £146 million, more than double the sales growth experienced by the major supermarkets. As we enter an age of unprecedented food insecurity, it is essential that our consumption reflects not only what is desirable, but also what is ultimately sustainable. While the 'organic' label itself may inevitably be hijacked, 'organic and local' represents a solution with which the global players can simply never compete.

EVALUATING THE AUTHORS' ARGUMENTS:

In this viewpoint Hamer and Anslow argue organic food saves energy by being farmed, produced, and sold locally. How do you think Field Maloney, author of the next viewpoint, would respond to this claim? After reading both viewpoints, what is your position on the issue of whether organic farming saves or wastes energy?

Viewpoint

4

Organic Farming Wastes Energy

Field Maloney

"Just think of the fossil fuels expended getting those organic tomatoes from Chile."

In the following viewpoint Field Maloney argues that organic farming wastes energy. If organic food is produced locally, Maloney agrees it can be environmentally friendly. But he claims that most of the organic food sold in the United States travels great distances to reach its customers. When food is transported, large amounts of fossil fuels are used and greenhouse gases are emitted. Organic food travels far because the farming techniques it requires cannot be used year-round in all places. As a result, local organic farmers provide very little of the food sold in large organic grocery stores. Maloney criticizes organic stores like Whole Foods for selling an environmentally friendly image, when in fact they hurt the environment by selling food that has been transported long distances.

Maloney is a writer whose articles have appeared on Slate.com.

AS YOU READ, CONSIDER THE FOLLOWING QUESTIONS:
1. According to the author, when is it better to buy conventionally grown tomatoes instead of organic tomatoes?
2. Where does Maloney say most of America's organic food comes from?
3. What problem does the author have with the "grower profiles" posted in the organic grocery store Whole Foods?

I t's hard to find fault with Whole Foods, the haute-crunchy supermarket chain that has made a fortune by transforming grocery shopping into a bright and shiny, progressive experience. Indeed, the road to wild profits and cultural cachet has been surprisingly smooth for the supermarket chain. It gets mostly sympathetic coverage in the local and national media and red-carpet treatment from the communities it enters. But does Whole Foods have an Achilles' heel? And more important, does the organic movement itself, whose coattails Whole Foods has ridden to such success, have dark secrets of its own?

The Organic Image

Granted, there's plenty that's praiseworthy about Whole Foods. John Mackey, the company's chairman, likes to say, "There's no inherent reason why business cannot be ethical, socially responsible, and profitable." And under the umbrella creed of "sustainability," Whole Foods pays its workers a solid living wage—its lowest earners average $13.15 an hour—with excellent benefits and health care. No executive makes more than 14 times the employee average. (Mackey's salary last year was $342,000.) In January [2006], Whole Foods announced that it had committed to buy a year's supply of power from a wind-power utility in Wyoming.

But even if Whole Foods has a happy staff and nice windmills, is it really as virtuous as it appears to be? Take the produce section, usually located in the geographic center of the shopping floor and the spiritual heart of a Whole Foods outlet. (Every media profile of the company invariably contains a paragraph of fawning produce porn, near-sonnets about "gleaming melons" and "glistening kumquats.") In the produce

Organic Farming and Climate Change

The process of farming organic foods emits only slightly less greenhouse gas than conventional crops, and the production of some items emit significantly more.

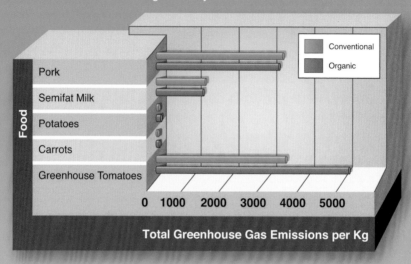

Taken from: Halberg 2008. International Centre for Research in Organic Food Systems.

section of Whole Foods' flagship New York City store at the Time Warner Center, shoppers browse under a big banner that lists "Reasons To Buy Organic." On the banner, the first heading is "Save Energy." The accompanying text explains how organic farmers, who use natural fertilizers like manure and compost, avoid the energy waste involved in the manufacture of synthetic fertilizers. It's a technical point that probably barely registers with most shoppers but contributes to a vague sense of virtue.

When Organic Food Travels It Wastes Energy

Fair enough. But here's another technical point that Whole Foods fails to mention and that highlights what has gone wrong with the organic-food movement in the last couple of decades. Let's say you live in New York City and want to buy a pound of tomatoes in season. Say you can choose between conventionally grown New Jersey tomatoes or organic ones grown in Chile. Of course, the New Jersey tomatoes will be cheaper. They will also almost certainly be fresher, having traveled a fraction of the distance. But which is the more eco-conscious choice? In terms of energy savings, there's no contest: Just think of the fossil fuels expended getting those organic tomatoes from Chile. Which brings us to the question: Setting aside freshness, price, and energy conservation, should a New Yorker just instinctively choose organic, even if the produce comes from Chile? A tough decision, but you can make a self-interested case for the social and economic benefit of going Jersey, especially if you prefer passing fields of tomatoes to fields of condominiums when you tour the Garden State.

Most Organic Food Is Not Local

Another heading on the Whole Foods banner says "Help the Small Farmer." "Buying organic," it states, "supports the small, family farmers that make up a large percentage of organic food producers." This is semantic sleight of hand. As one small family farmer in Connecticut told me recently, "Almost all the organic food in this country comes out of California. And five or six big California farms dominate the whole industry." There's a widespread misperception in this country—one that organic growers, no matter how giant, happily encourage—that "organic" means "small family farmer." That hasn't been the case for years, certainly not since 1990, when the Department of Agriculture drew up its official guidelines for organic food. Whole Foods knows this well, and so the line about the "small family farmers that make up a large percentage of organic food producers" is sneaky.

> **FAST FACT**
>
> A 2007 study by researchers at the University of Alberta in Canada found that transporting twenty tons of organic produce grown far from a market emitted the same amount of greenhouse gases as conventional fruit and vegetables grown nearby.

There are a lot of small, family-run organic farmers, but their share of the organic crop in this country, and of the produce sold at Whole Foods, is minuscule.

A nearby banner at the Time Warner Center Whole Foods proclaims "Our Commitment to the Local Farmer," but this also doesn't hold up to scrutiny. More likely, the burgeoning local-food movement is making Whole Foods uneasy. After all, a multinational chain can't promote a "buy local" philosophy without being self-defeating. When I visited the Time Warner Whole Foods last fall—high season for native fruits and vegetables on the East Coast—only a token amount of local produce was on display. What Whole Foods does do for local farmers is hang glossy pinups throughout the store, what they call "grower profiles," which depict tousled, friendly looking organic farmers standing in front of their crops. This winter, when I dropped by the store, the only local produce for sale was a shelf of upstate apples, but the grower profiles were still up. There was a picture of a sandy-haired organic leek farmer named Dave, from Whately, Mass., above a shelf of conventionally grown yellow onions from Oregon. Another profile showed a guy named Ray Rex munching on an ear of sweet corn he grew on his generations-old, picturesque organic acres. The photograph was pinned above a display of conventionally grown white onions from Mexico.

These profiles may be heartwarming, but they also artfully mislead customers about what they're paying premium prices for. If Whole Foods marketing didn't revolve so much around explicit (as well as subtly suggestive) appeals to food ethics, it'd be easier to forgive some exaggerations and distortions.

Not Local, but Certainly Elitist

Of course, above and beyond social and environmental ethics, and even taste, people buy organic food because they believe that it's better for them. All things being equal, food grown without pesticides is healthier for you. But American populism chafes against the notion of good health for those who can afford it. Charges of elitism—media wags, in otherwise flattering profiles, have called Whole Foods "Whole Paycheck" and "wholesome, healthy for the wholesome, wealthy"—are the only criticism of Whole Foods that seems to have stuck. Which brings us to the newest kid in the organic-food sandbox: Wal-Mart, the world's biggest grocery retailer, has just begun a major program to expand into organic foods. If buying food grown without chemical pesticides and synthetic fertilizers has been elevated to a status-conscious lifestyle choice, it could also be transformed into a bare-bones commodity purchase.

The author argues that Whole Foods' organic produce imports waste energy because of long-distance shipping.

When the Department of Agriculture established the guidelines for organic food in 1990, it blew a huge opportunity. The USDA—under heavy agribusiness lobbying—adopted an abstract set of restrictions for organic agriculture and left "local" out of the formula. What passes for organic farming today has strayed far from what the shaggy utopians who got the movement going back in the '60s and '70s had in mind. But if these pioneers dreamed of revolutionizing the nation's food supply, they surely didn't intend for organic to become a luxury item, a high-end lifestyle choice.

It's likely that neither Wal-Mart nor Whole Foods will do much to encourage local agriculture or small farming, but in an odd twist, Wal-Mart, with its simple "More for Less" credo, might do far more to democratize the nation's food supply than Whole Foods. The organic-food movement is in danger of exacerbating the growing gap between rich and poor in this country by contributing to a two-tiered national food supply, with healthy food for the rich. Could Wal-Mart's populist strategy prove to be more "sustainable" than Whole Foods? Stranger things have happened.

EVALUATING THE AUTHOR'S ARGUMENTS:

Maloney accuses stores like Whole Foods of deceiving their customers. What do you think he means by this? Explain what you think he is implying, and then state whether you agree.

Organic Food Can Solve World Hunger

Brian Halweil

"A large scale shift to organic farming would not only increase the world's food supply, but might be the only way to eradicate hunger."

In the following viewpoint Brian Halweil argues that organic farming techniques can increase the world's food supply and may even produce enough food to eradicate hunger. He says it is often assumed that organic farming produces lower levels of food than conventional farming. Yet studies from the University of Michigan and other institutes have shown that when done according to certain models, organic farming can produce as many, or even 75 percent more, of the food calories per person that conventional farming techniques can. He says that organic farming techniques can especially reduce hunger in Third World places like Africa and Asia, where soil is poor and citizens cannot afford to import expensive food from other countries. Halweil encourages world leaders to consider organic farming as a solution to world hunger and poverty.

Halweil is a senior researcher at the Worldwatch Institute and the author of *Eat Here: Reclaiming Homegrown Pleasures in a Global Supermarket.*

AS YOU READ, CONSIDER THE FOLLOWING QUESTIONS:
  1. How many calories per person did an optimistic organic farming model find it possible to produce, as reported by the author?
  2. On what three poverty-stricken continents does Halweil say organic farming could produce more food?
  3. In what way does Halweil report organic farming can contribute to "rural stability"?

The only people who think organic farming can feed the world are delusional hippies, hysterical moms, and self-righteous organic farmers, right?

Actually, no. A fair number of agribusiness executives, agricultural and ecological scientists, and international agriculture experts believe that a large scale shift to organic farming would not only increase the world's food supply, but might be the only way to eradicate hunger.

Studying Organic Farming Yields

[In 2006] inspired by a field trip to a nearby organic farm where the farmer reported he raised an amazing 27 tons of vegetables on six-tenths of an hectare [a metric unit of land measurement; one hectare equals about 2.5 acres] in a relatively short growing season, a team of scientists from the University of Michigan tried to estimate how much food could be raised following a global shift to organic farming.

The team combed through the literature for any and all studies comparing crop yields on organic farms with those on non-organic farms. Based on 293 examples, they came up with a global dataset of yield ratios for the world's major crops for the developed and the developing world.

As expected, organic farming yielded less than conventional farming in the developed world (where farmers use copious amounts of synthetic fertilizers and pesticides in a perennial attempt to maximize yields), while studies from the developing world showed organic farming boosted yields. (Examples from growing areas as diverse as India, Guatemala, and Kenya found that the sophisticated combination of old wisdom and modern ecological innovations that help harness the yield-boosting effects of cover crops, compost, manure, beneficial insects, and crop synergies in organic farming were particularly useful in dry areas with poor soils where farmers aren't likely to afford agrochemicals any time soon).

Organic Farming Can Produce More Food Calories

The team then ran two models. The first was conservative, and the second was optimistic, based on yield gaps between organic and nonorganic practices in developed and developing countries.

The first model yielded 2,641 kilocalories per person per day, just under the world's current production of 2,786 calories but significantly higher than the average caloric requirement for a healthy person of between 2,200 and 2,500. The second model yielded 4,381

A farmer picks vegetables at an organic farm in India. The author says that old wisdom and modern organic farming techniques are increasing crop yield in that nation.

calories per person per day, 75% greater than current availability—and a quantity that could theoretically sustain a much larger human population than is currently supported on the world's farmland.

A second recent study of the potential of a global shift to organic farming, led by Niels Halberg of the Danish Institute of Agricultural Sciences, came to very similar conclusions, even though the authors were economists, agronomists, and international development experts.

Organic Farming Can Feed People in Poor Countries

Like the Michigan team, Halberg's group made an assumption about the differences in yields with organic farming for a range of crops, and then plugged those numbers into a model developed by the World Bank's International Food Policy Research Institute. This model is considered the definitive algorithm for predicting food output, farm income and the number of hungry people throughout the world.

Given the growing interest in organic farming among consumers, government officials, and agricultural scientists, the researchers wanted to assess whether a large-scale conversion to organic farming in Europe and North America (the world's primary food exporting regions) would reduce yields, increase world food prices, or worsen hunger in poorer nations that depend on imports, particularly people living in the Third World's swelling mega-cities.

Although the group found that total food production declined in Europe and North America, the model didn't show a substantial impact on world food prices. And because the model assumed, like the Michigan study, that organic farming would boost yields in Africa, Asia and Latin America, the most optimistic scenario even had hunger-plagued sub-Saharan Africa exporting food surpluses. In other words, studies from the field show that the yield increases from

> **FAST FACT**
>
> According to a study by the Rodale Institute, organic crops produced the same amount of food as conventional crops over a twenty-year period. Furthermore, organic yielded 28 to 34 percent more food than conventional crops in drought conditions.

Organic Crops Produce as Much Food as Conventional Crops

A ten-year study of crop yields in Öjebyn, Sweden, found that organic crops yielded as much or more food as conventional crops. Supporters say organic food could play a role in reducing hunger around the world.

Total Crop Yields, 1990–2000

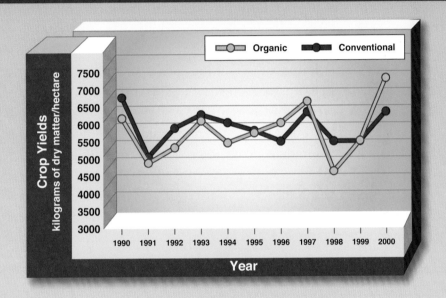

Taken from: Simon Johnson, Swedish University of Agricultural Sciences, 2002.

shifting to organic farming are highest and most consistent in exactly those poor, dry, remote areas where hunger is most severe.

But even some supporters of organic farming shy away from asking whether it can feed the world, because they don't think it's the most useful question. First, even if a mass conversion over, say, the next two decades, dramatically increased food production, there's little guarantee it would eradicate hunger. The global food system can be a complex and unpredictable beast. It's hard to anticipate how China's rise as a major importer of soybeans for its feedlots, for instance, might affect food supplies elsewhere (It's likely to drive up food prices). Or how elimination of agricultural subsidies in wealthy nations might affect poorer countries (It's likely to boost farm incomes and reduce hunger). And would less meat eating around the world free up food for the hungry? (It would, but could the hungry afford it?)

Organic Farming Has Many Social Benefits

What is clear is that organic farming will yield other benefits that are too numerous to name. Studies have shown, for example, that the "external" costs of organic farming—erosion, chemical pollution to drinking water, death of birds and other wildlife—are just one-third those of conventional farming. Surveys from every continent show that organic farms support many more species of birds, wild plants, insects and other wildlife than conventional farms.

And tests by several governments have shown that organic foods carry just a tiny fraction of the pesticide residues of their non-organic alternatives, while completely banning growth hormones, antibiotics, and many additives allowed in many conventional foods.

There is even some evidence that crops grown organically have considerably higher levels of health-promoting antioxidants. A recent study by the International Fund for Agricultural Development found that the higher labor requirements often mean that "organic agriculture can prove particularly effective in bringing redistribution of resources in areas where the labor force is underemployed. This can help contribute to rural stability."

The Myth of Low-Yield Organic Farming

These benefits will come even without a complete conversion to a sort of organic utopia. In fact, some experts think that a more hopeful, and reasonable, way forward is a sort of middle ground, where more and more farmers adopt the principles of organic farming even if they don't follow the approach religiously. In this scenario, both poor farmers and the environment come out way ahead. And it's likely that the greatest short-term benefits will come as the principles of organic farming rub off on non-organic farmers, who will come to depend on just a small fraction of the chemicals they currently use.

Anywhere this middle path is adopted, pollution will go down, and yields will go up. And, since it will cost farmers less than the full-blown conversion, many more regions will likely adopt it.

So, the myth of low-yielding organic farming may be fading, but without a massive change of conscience from the world's agricultural researchers and officials, we still won't be pointed in the organic direction. And that could be the real problem for the world's poor and hungry.

EVALUATING THE AUTHOR'S ARGUMENTS:

In this viewpoint Halweil suggests organic farming can feed the world. What key pieces of evidence does he provide to support this claim? List at least three of them. Did he convince you of his argument? Explain why or why not.

Viewpoint

6

Organic Food Cannot Solve World Hunger

Dennis T. Avery and Alex A. Avery

"You cannot feed six billion people today and nine billion in 2050 without judicious use of chemical fertilizers."

In the following viewpoint Dennis T. Avery and Alex A. Avery argue that organic farming cannot feed the world. They take issue with studies that argue that organic food is a solution to hunger, arguing these studies are methodologically flawed. In their opinion, organic farming simply cannot yield the amount of food that is needed to feed the world. Furthermore, the world's population is expected to grow so much that conventional methods can barely handle the additional load, let alone organic methods, which require more land and more resources such as water. Finally, organic farming techniques would require that many acres of farmland be used to generate nonfood items, such as manure for natural fertilization. The authors urge world leaders and scientists to stop pushing the idea that organic farming can help eradicate world hunger—relying on organic farming is likely to produce less food and make less farmland available for crops, in their opinion.

Dennis T. Avery and Alex A. Avery, "New Year's Resolution: Organic Farming Can't Feed the World," Center for Global Food Issues, January 3, 2006. Reproduced by permission.

Dennis T. Avery is a senior fellow at the Hudson Institute. Alex A. Avery is a plant physiologist and director of research at the Hudson Institute's Center for Global Food Issues.

AS YOU READ, CONSIDER THE FOLLOWING QUESTIONS:
1. According to Avery and Avery, what is the UN Food and Agriculture Organization's opinion on whether organic crops can feed the world?
2. What specific criticisms do the authors have of a University of Michigan study that claimed organic farming could feed the world?
3. Who is Kip Cullers and how does he factor into the authors' argument?

W e're already sacrificing our energy sources to "save the planet." Now the Greens want us to give up food as well.

The Lie That Organic Farmers Tell

Last summer [in 2007], a University of Michigan study announced that "organic farming can feed the world." "My hope is that we can finally put a nail in the coffin of the idea that you can't produce enough food through organic agriculture," said co-author Ivette Perfecto.

Not even the United Nations believes this fabrication. The UN Food and Agriculture Organization

> **FAST FACT**
>
> According to a twenty-one-year study by the Research Institute for Organic Agriculture, organic farm plots are on average 20 percent less productive than conventional plots. For potatoes, organic production is about 40 percent lower.

just released a statement saying, "FAO has no reason to believe that organic agriculture can substitute for conventional farming systems in ensuring the world's food security." Director-General Jaques Diouf said, "you cannot feed six billion people today and nine billion in 2050 without judicious use of chemical fertilizers."

Organic Farming Wastes Land

The share of farmland used for organic production has increased in many rich countries. But as global food prices soar, hurting the poor in particular, some say organic farming should be abandoned since it produces far less than conventional intensive methods, and so more land must be farmed for the same yield.

Organic Land Management

Share of agricultural land area under certified organic management, selected countries, 2002–04, in percentages

Organic Cannot Meet the Growing Demand

The food question is critical, since a peak population of 9 billion humans will apparently demand more than twice as much farm output by 2050. Already, the world's farmers are using 40 percent of the planet's land area. Clearing forests to double cropland would crowd out many thousands of wild species.

How can the Michigan and the FAO organic assessments be so far apart? Know that the U-M doesn't have a school of agriculture. The paper's lead author, Catherine Badgley, is a geologist.

The "breakthrough study" was compiled from secondary sources—few of them based on actual organic farming.

Misunderstanding What Organic Means

U-M reported 37 percent higher Argentine corn yields from organic. But that report came from an Argentine farmer named Roberto Peiretti—a friend of mine and a famous no-till farmer.[1] No-till always uses herbicides for weed control. Roberto also uses industrial fertilizers, pesticides and biotech seeds. In fact, nearly 100 of the studies the U-M authors claimed as "organic" were not.

The U-M response? "We used a broader meaning of organic . . . so that we could legitimately include studies that involve practices that are substantially in the direction of strict organic."

No-till is never organic. USDA researchers have spent ten years trying to create a no-till system for organic farmers, because no-till is so effective at stopping soil erosion. They've failed. Apparently, the U-M authors wanted to claim high yields for political purposes.

Organic Farms Take Up Too Much Land

Fertilizer, of course, is the biggest difference between organic and conventional farming. Unfortunately, the world has only one-fourth of the animal manure needed to supply N [nitrogen] for the world's crops.

Badgley and Perfecto say ". . . we present data from temperate and tropical agroecosystems showing that leguminous cover crops grown

1. No-till farming is a technique in which soil is not regularly turned.

Missouri farmer Kip Gullers shows off his record-yielding soybean fields to farmers. He uses irrigation and lots of fungicide and fertilizer to achieve the yield.

between normal cropping periods could fix more nitrogen than all the synthetic nitrogen currently in use."

Their own paper, however, warns that green manure crops sacrifice food yields. A long-term California test reported favorable organic wheat yields—but Badgley and Perfecto failed to tell us about a 50 percent reduction in yield for the following corn crop. The corn had to be planted late—so the green manure crop could mature. There are few farms in the world where green manure crops don't take field time, sunlight and water away from the food/feed crops.

Our answer to "organic can feed the world"? Missouri farmer Kip Cullers, who has gotten 154 bushels per acre of soybeans (U.S.

average 41 bu.) and 347 bushels of corn per acre (U.S. average 156 bu.). Cullers achieves this on irrigated plots with lots of fungicides and fertilizer—but that's instructive about conventional farming's potential to feed the world and save wildlands from plowdown.

EVALUATING THE AUTHORS' ARGUMENTS:

In this viewpoint the authors take issue with a 2007 University of Michigan study that claimed organic farming can feed the world. Brian Halweil discussed the same study in the previous viewpoint, except he supported the study's conclusion. After reading both viewpoints' characterizations, what is your opinion of the University of Michigan study? How did you arrive at your point of view?

Chapter 3

What Is the Future of Organic Food?

Organic brands of food are increasingly being carried in both small, locally owned stores and national grocery chains— but not all products labeled "organic" are equal.

Organic Food Is a Passing Fad

Brian Dunning

"When the major food producers saw that organic food was coming into vogue . . . they smelled higher prices."

In the following viewpoint Brian Dunning argues that organic food is a trend that should go out of style. He claims that people who believe organic food is better for them and the environment have been deceived—most organic food is produced by the same companies that make conventional food, and there is no evidence to show it is any more healthful. Companies have figured out people will pay top dollar for anything labeled organic, and Dunning says people who fall for the scam of organic food are wasting their money. Dunning urges people to realize that expensive organic food does not actually come from small, local, organic family farms but from large corporations who want to earn huge profits on the latest hot items.

Dunning is the host and producer of the weekly podcast *Skeptoid*.

AS YOU READ, CONSIDER THE FOLLOWING QUESTIONS:
1. What percentage of all organic milk is controlled by one major milk producer, according to Dunning?

2. Who is Theo Albrecht, and how does he factor into the author's argument?

3. What does Dunning say about the reason organic farming is practiced in China?

Today we're going to put on our tie dyed shirt, grow our hair long and dirty, claim hatred for science and corporate America, then walk into the most expensive specialty supermarket in town and purchase one of the most overpriced products on the market today: Organic food.

Organic Food Is Still Just Food

Organic food is a conventional food crop (genetically exactly the same plant variety as the regular version) but grown according to a different set of standards. In this sense, organic food is really the same thing as kosher food. The food itself is identical, but it's prepared in such a way to conform to different philosophical standards. Just as kosher standards are defined by rabbinical authorities, the USDA's National Organic Program sets the requirements for foods to bear a "certified organic" label. Basically it forbids the use of modern synthetic fertilizers and pesticides in favor of organic equivalents, and for animals it requires that they have not been kept healthy through the use of antibiotics. There are other rules too, and the basic goal is to require the use of only natural products throughout the growth, preparation, and preservation stages.

Organic food is more expensive than conventional food, due not only to its lower crop yields and more expensive organic fertilizers and pesticides in larger quantities, but mainly because it's such a big fad right now and is in such high demand. . . .

Making Big Bucks

Make no mistake, organic food is big, big business. The days when the organic produce section of the supermarket represented the product of a small local farmer are long gone. California alone produces over $600 million in organic produce, most of it coming from just five farms, who are also the same producers of most non-organic food in

The author says Trader Joe's, a national supermarket chain that markets itself as an organic, environmentally friendly, and small business–type of store, is no different than conventional food sellers.

the state. Seventy percent of all organic milk is controlled by just one major milk producer.

Five or ten years ago, when the major food producers saw that organic food was coming into vogue, what do you think they did? They smelled higher prices charged for less product, and started producing organic crops. Nearly all organic crops in the United States are either grown, distributed, or sold by exactly the same companies who produce conventional crops. They don't care which one you buy. You're not striking a blow at anyone, except at your own pocketbook.

Organic Food Sellers Are Just Like Conventional Food Sellers

Trader Joe's is a supermarket chain specializing in organic, vegetarian, and alternative foods with hundreds of locations throughout the United States, centered in organic-happy Southern California. Shoppers appreciate its image of healthful food in a small-business

"This new grocery store is divided into two sections: organic and things I can afford."

"This new grocery store is divided into two sections: organic and things I can afford," cartoon by Chris Wildt. www.CartoonStock.com. © Chris Wildt. Reproduction rights obtainable from www.CartoonStock.com.

family atmosphere. Really? In 2005 alone, Trader Joe's racked up sales estimated at $4.5 billion. The company is owned by a family trust set up by German billionaire Theo Albrecht, ranked the 22nd richest man in the world by *Forbes* in 2004. He's the co-founder and CEO of German multi-national ALDI, with global revenue in grocery sales at $37 billion. According to *Business Week*, the decade of the 1990's saw Trader Joe's increase its profits by 1000%. Trader Joe's also compensates its employees aggressively, with starting salaries for supervisors at $40,000. They hire only non-union workers. Now, to any capitalist or business-minded person, there's nothing wrong with any of that (unless you're pro-union or anti-

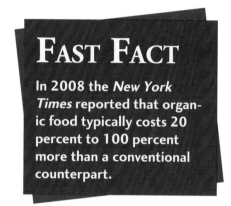

FAST FACT

In 2008 the *New York Times* reported that organic food typically costs 20 percent to 100 percent more than a conventional counterpart.

big business). It's a great company, and very successful. Trader Joe's customers are willing to pay their premium prices to get that beautiful image, but they should not kid themselves that they're striking a blow at big business and supporting the little guy.

I'm not exactly sure why anticorporatism wound up on the organic food agenda, since it's so counterintuitive. The irony is that the organic food companies supply a smaller amount of food per acre planted, and enjoy dramatically higher profits, which is why anticorporatists hate corporations in the first place. . . .

There Is No Reason to Buy Organic

Did you ever wonder why Chinese drink only hot tea? They boil it to kill the bacteria. Most local Chinese farming uses organic methods, in that the only fertilizers used are human and animal waste: Without being boiled, it's basically a nice cup of E. coli. In the case of China and other poor Asian nations, the reason for organic farming has less to do with ideology and more to do with lack of access to modern farming technology.

The *National Review* reports that Americans believe organic food is healthier by a 2-1 margin, despite the lack of any evidence supporting this. When you take the exact same strain of a plant and grow it in two different ways, its chemical and genetic makeup remain the same. One may be larger than the other if one growing method was more efficient, but its fundamental makeup and biochemical content is defined by its genes, not by the way it was grown. *Consumer Reports* found no consistent difference in appearance, flavor, or texture. A blanket statement like "organic cultivation results in a crop with superior nutritional value" has no logical or factual basis. . . .

The Dirty Secret About Organic Farming

Organic methods require about twice the acreage to produce the same crop, thus directly resulting in the destruction of undeveloped land. During a recent Girl Scout field trip to Tanaka Farms in Irvine, California, one of the owners told us his dirty little secret that contradicts what you'll find on his web site. Market conditions compelled them to switch to organic a few years ago, and he absolutely hates it. The per-acre yield has been slashed. Organic farming produces less food, and requires more acreage.

Many so-called environmentalists generally favor organic farming, at the same time that they protest deforestation to make room for more agriculture. How do they reconcile these directly conflicting views? If you want to feed a growing population, you *cannot do* both, and soon won't be able to do either. If you support rainforest preservation, logically you should oppose organic farming, particularly in the developing world. On the other hand, if you demand organic soybeans, then you should have the courage to stand up and say that you don't care whether black and brown people around the world have enough to eat or not.

I'm not making this stuff up. For every dreadlocked white kid beating a bongo drum in favor of organics, there is a Ph.D. agriculturist warning about its short sightedness and urging efficient modern agriculture to feed our growing population. Personally I like forests and natural areas, so I favor using the farmlands that we *already* have as efficiently as possible. This benefits everyone. I say we dump the useless paranormal objections to foods freighted with evil corporate hate energy, and instead use our brains to our advantage for once. When we find a better way to grow the same crop faster, stronger, healthier, and on less acreage, let's do it. We all benefit.

EVALUATING THE AUTHOR'S ARGUMENTS:

To make his argument that organic food is not really that different from regular food, Brian Dunning compares it to kosher food. Explain the comparison he makes. In what way does he think organic food is like kosher food? Given what you know on the topic, do you think this is a fair comparison? Why or why not?

Organic Food Is the Diet of the Future

Libby Quaid

> *"America's appetite for organic food is so strong that supply just can't keep up with demand."*

The demand for organic food is growing and shows no signs of slowing down, Libby Quaid argues in the following viewpoint. She asserts that organic food is not a passing fad and discusses how growing numbers of people are looking to organic food for dietary, environmental, and political reasons. She explains that demand for organic food has become so great, organic ingredients are in short supply. In fact, more organic farms are needed to supply organic food makers with the ingredients they need. Quaid predicts that organic farmers and food makers will experience tremendous growth in coming years as a result of the here-to-stay popularity of organic foods.

Quaid is a reporter whose articles have appeared in the *Examiner,* the *Los Angeles Times,* and the Associated Press.

AS YOU READ, CONSIDER THE FOLLOWING QUESTIONS:

1. By what percentage does Quaid say organic food sales grow each year? How does that compare with total food sales?

2. How many organic farms exist in America today, according to the author?
3. How are organic companies like Stonyfield and Organic Valley working to increase the number of organic farms, as reported by Quaid?

America's appetite for organic food is so strong that supply just can't keep up with demand. Organic products still have only a tiny slice, about 2.5 percent, of the nation's food market. But the slice is expanding at a feverish pace.

The Growing Interest in Organic Food

Growth in sales of organic food has been 15 percent to 21 percent each year, compared with 2 percent to 4 percent for total food sales.

Organic means food is grown without bug killer, fertilizer, hormones, antibiotics or biotechnology.

Mainstream supermarkets, eyeing the success of organic retailers such as Whole Foods, have rushed to meet demand. The Kroger Co., Safeway Inc. and SuperValu Inc., which owns Albertson's LLC, are among those selling their own organic brands. Wal-Mart Stores Inc. said earlier this year it would double its organic offerings.

FAST FACT

The Organic Trade Association reports that annual sales of organic food and beverages grew from $1 billion in 1990 to well over $20 billion in 2007.

The number of organic farms— an estimated 10,000—is also increasing, but not fast enough. As a result, organic manufacturers are looking for ingredients outside the United States in places like Europe, Bolivia, Venezuela and South Africa.

Organic Companies Are Trying to Keep Up with Demand

That is no surprise, said Barbara Robinson, head of the Agriculture Department's National Organic Program. The program provides the round, green "USDA Organic" seal for certified products.

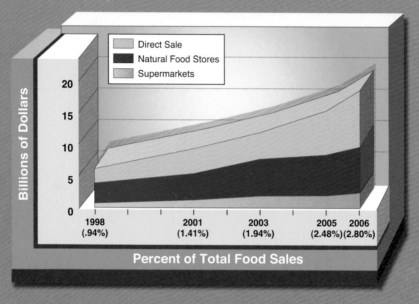

Organic Food Is Big Business

Sales of organic food in the United States have increased about 20 percent each year since 1990.

Billions of Dollars

Direct Sale
Natural Food Stores
Supermarkets

20
15
10
5
0

| 1998 | 2001 | 2003 | 2005 | 2006 |
| (.94%) | (1.41%) | (1.94%) | (2.48%) | (2.80%) |

Percent of Total Food Sales

Taken from: Organic Trade Association, 2007.

Her agency is just now starting to track organic data, but Robinson believes the United States is importing far more organic food than it exports. That's true of conventional food, too.

"That is how you stimulate growth, is imports generally," she said. "Your own industry says we're tired of importing this; why should I pay for imports when I could start producing myself?"

"We're doing a lot of scrambling," said Sheryl O'Loughlin, CEO of Clif Bar Inc. "We have gotten to the point now where we know we can get a call for any ingredient."

The makers of the high-energy, eat-and-run Clif Bar needed 85,000 pounds of almonds, and they had to be organic. But the nation's organic almond crop was spoken for. Eventually, Clif Bar found the almonds—in Spain. But more shortages have popped up: apricots and blueberries, cashews and hazelnuts, brown rice syrup and oats.

Even Stonyfield Farm, an organic pioneer in the United States, is pursuing a foreign supplier; Stonyfield is working on a deal to import milk powder from New Zealand.

"I'm not suggesting we would be importing from all these places," said Gary Hirshberg, president and CEO of Stonyfield Farm Inc. "But for transition purposes, to help organic supply to keep up with the nation's growing hunger, these countries have to be considered."

Organic Is a Way of Life

The dilemma of how to fill the gap between organic supply and demand is part of a long-running debate within America's booming organic industry. For many enthusiasts, organic is about more than the food on their plates; it's a way to improve the environment where they live and help keep small-scale farmers in business.

"If organic is something created in the image of sustainable agriculture, we certainly haven't accomplished that yet," said Urvashi Rangan, a scientist for Consumers Union. "What people do have to understand is if that stuff comes in from overseas, and it's got an organic label on it, it had to meet USDA standards in order to get here."

The issue causes mixed feelings for Travis Forgues, an organic dairy farmer in Vermont. "I don't like the idea of it coming in from

Organic Valley's new $5.9 million headquarters in LaFarge, Wisconsin is testimony to the rising profitability of organic products in the United States.

out of this country, but I don't want them to stop growing organic because of that," Forgues said. "I want people to say, 'Let's do that here, give a farmer another avenue to make a livable wage.'" A member of the farmer-owned Organic Valley cooperative, Forgues got his dairy farm certified nearly 10 years ago. Organic Valley supplies milk to Stonyfield.

Switching to organic is a difficult proposition. Vegetable grower Scott Woodard is learning through trial and error on his Putnam Valley, N.Y., farm. One costly mistake: Conventional farmers can plant seeds when they want and use pesticides to kill hungry insect larvae. If Woodard had waited three weeks to plant, the bugs that ate his seeds would have hatched and left. Organic seeds can be double the price of conventional.

"There's not a lot of information out there," Woodard said. "We try to do the best we can. Sometimes it's too late, but then we learn for next time."

More Organic Farms Are Needed

Stonyfield and Organic Valley are working to increase the number of organic farms, paying farmers to help them switch or boost production. Stonyfield, together with farmer-owned cooperative Organic Valley, expects to spend around $2 million on incentives and technical help in 2006, Hirshberg said.

Other companies offer similar help. And the industry's Organic Trade Association is trying to become more of a resource for individual farmers.

Caren Wilcox, the group's executive director, described how an Illinois farmer showed up in May at an industry show in Chicago. "He said, 'I want to get certified. Help me,'" Wilcox said. "It was a smart thing to do, but the fact that he had to get into his car and go down to McCormick Center says something about the availability of information."

In the meantime, manufacturers like Clif Bar and Stonyfield still prefer to buy organic ingredients, wherever they come from, instead of conventional crops in the U.S. "Anybody who's helping to take toxins out of the biosphere and use less poisonous chemicals in agriculture is a hero of mine," Hirshberg said. "There's enormous opportunity here for everybody to win, large and small."

EVALUATING THE AUTHORS' ARGUMENTS:

Libby Quaid and Brian Dunning (author of the previous viewpoint) disagree on whether organic food is a passing fad or the diet of the future. What do you think? Have you ever eaten any organic food? Are you interested in making it a larger part of your diet? Why or why not? Explain your reasoning.

Organic Food Should Not Be Sold in Chain Stores

"To say you can sell organic food for 10 percent above the price at which you sell irresponsibly priced food suggests you don't really get it."

Michael Pollan

In the following viewpoint Michael Pollan discusses why he thinks chain stores seeking to sell organic food threaten the very foundation of the organic movement. He argues that when organic food is produced in mass quantities, it adopts similar qualities to conventional food. For example, to mass produce organic milk, one must house cattle away from their natural habitat and feed them something other than their natural diet. To mass produce organic fruits and vegetables, one must use large amounts of pesticides and fertilizers, calling into question whether such growing methods are natural or not. Such food production operations may be technically "organic," but in Pollan's view they are still factories that betray the organic movement's original instinct to produce food locally and in harmony with natural systems. He concludes that big retailers like Wal-Mart are likely to pervert the qualities of organic food that make it organic in the first place.

Michael Pollan has written several books about food and farming, including *In Defense of Food* and *The Omnivore's Dilemma*.

AS YOU READ, CONSIDER THE FOLLOWING QUESTIONS:
1. According to the author, what should the motto of America's food system be?
2. What problem does Pollan have with organic dairies located in the desert?
3. How does Pollan say big organic meat producers satisfy the requirement that organically raised animals must have access to the outdoors?

At the risk of sounding more equivocal than any self-respecting blogger is expected to sound, I'm going to turn my attention from the benefits of Wal-Mart's decision to enter the organic food market to its costs. You'll have to decide for yourself whether the advantage of making organic food accessible to more Americans is outweighed by the damage Wal-Mart may do to the practice and meaning of organic food production. The trade-offs are considerable.

When Wal-Mart announced its plan to offer consumers a wide selection of organic foods, the company claimed it would keep the price premium for organic to no more than 10 percent. This in itself is grounds for concern—in my view, it virtually guarantees that Wal-Mart's version of cheap, industrialized organic food will not be sustainable in any meaningful sense of the word (see my earlier column, "Voting With Your Fork," for a discussion of that word). Why? Because to index the price of organic to the price of conventional food is to give up, right from the start, on the idea—once enshrined in the organic movement—that food should be priced responsibly. Cheap industrial food, the organic movement has argued, only seems cheap, because the real costs are charged to the environment (in the form of water and air pollution and depletion of the soil); to the public purse (in the form of subsidies to conventional commodity producers); and to the public health (in the cost of diabetes, obesity and cardiovascular disease), not to mention to the welfare of the farm- and food-factory workers and the well-being of the animals. As Wendell Berry once wrote, the motto of our conventional food system—at the center of which stands Wal-Mart, the biggest grocer in America—should be: Cheap at Any Price!

To say you can sell organic food for 10 percent above the price at which you sell irresponsibly priced food suggests you don't really get it—that you plan to bring the same principles of industrial "efficiency" and "economies of scale" to a system of food production that was supposed to mimic the logic of nature rather than that of the factory.

We have already seen what happens when the logic of industry is applied to organic food production. Synthetic pesticides are simply replaced by approved organic pesticides; synthetic fertilizer is simply replaced by compost and manures and mined forms of nitrogen imported from South America. The result is a greener factory farm, to be sure, but a factory nevertheless.

The industrialization of organic agriculture, which Wal-Mart's entry will hasten, has given us "organic feedlots"—two words that I never thought would find their way into the same clause. To supply the burgeoning demand for cheap organic milk, agribusiness companies are setting up 5000-head dairies, often in the desert. The milking cows never touch a blade of grass, but instead spend their lives standing around a dry lot "loafing area" munching organic grain—grain that takes a toll on both the animals' health (these ruminants evolved to eat grass after all) and the nutritional value of their milk. Frequently the milk is then ultra-pasteurized (a high heat process that further diminishes its nutritional value) before being shipped across the country. This is the sort of milk we're going to see a lot more of in our supermarkets, as long as Wal-Mart honors its commitment to keep organic milk cheap.

We're also going to see more organic milk coming from places like New Zealand, a trend driven by soaring demand—and also by what seems to me, in an era of energy scarcity, a rather forgiving construc-

Organically grown lemons on display at Wal-Mart. The author argues that Wal-Mart and other big retailers are likely to dilute the quality of organic products.

tion of the idea of sustainability. Making organic food inexpensive means buying it from anywhere it can be produced most cheaply— lengthening rather than shortening the food chain, and deepening its dependence on fossil fuels.

Similarly, organic meat is increasingly coming not from polycultures growing a variety of species (which are able to recycle nutrients between plants and animals) but from ever-bigger organic confined animal feeding operations, or CAFO's, that, apart from not using antibiotics and feeding organic grain, are little different from their conventional counterparts. Yes, the organic rules say the animals should have "access to the outdoors," but in practice this means providing them with a tiny exercise yard or, in the case of one egg producer in New England, a screened-in concrete "porch." This is one of the ironies of practicing organic agriculture on an industrial scale: big, single-species organic CAFO's are even more precarious than their industrial cousins, since they can't rely on antibiotics to keep thousands of animals living in close confinement from getting sick. So organic CAFO-hands (to call them farm-hands just doesn't seem right) keep the free-ranging to a minimum, and then keep their fingers crossed.

The industrial food chain, whether organic or conventional, inevitably links giant supermarkets to giant farms. But this is not because big farms are any more efficient or productive than small farms—to the contrary. Studies have found that small farms produce more food per unit of land than big farms do). And polycultures are more productive than monocultures. So why don't such farms predominate? Because big supermarkets prefer to do business with big farms growing lots of the same thing. It is more efficient for Wal-Mart—in the economic, not the biological, sense—to contract with a single huge carrot or chicken grower than with 10 small ones: the "transaction costs" are lower, even if the price and the quality is no different. This is just one of the many ways in which the logic of capitalism and the logic of biology on a farm come into conflict. At least in the short term, the logic of business usually prevails.

Wal-Mart's big-foot entry into the organic market is bad news for small organic farmers, that seems obvious enough. But it may also spell trouble for the big growers they'll favor. Wal-Mart has a reputation for driving down prices by squeezing its suppliers, especially after the suppliers have invested in expanding production to feed the Wal-Mart maw. Once you've boosted your production to supply Wal-Mart, you're at the company's mercy when it decides it no longer wants to give you a price that will cover the cost of production, let alone enable you to make a profit. When that happens, the notion of responsibly priced food will be sacrificed to the need to survive, and the pressure to cut corners will become irresistible.

Right now, the federal organic standards provide a bulwark against that pressure. But with the industrialization of organic, the rules are coming under increasing pressure, and (forgive my skepticism) it's hard to believe that the lobbyists from Wal-Mart are going to play a constructive role in defending those standards from efforts to dilute them. Earlier this year, the Organic Trade Association hired lobbyists from Kraft to move a bill through Congress making it easier to include synthetic ingredients in products labeled organic.

(What are any synthetic ingredients doing in products labeled organic, anyway? A good question, and one that was recently posed in a lawsuit against the U.S. Department of Agriculture by a blueberry farmer in Maine, who argued that the 1990 law establishing the federal organic program had specifically prohibited synthetics in organic food. Within weeks after he won his case, the industry went to Congress to preserve its right to put synthetic ingredients like xanthan gum and ascorbic acid into organic processed foods.)

For better or worse, the legal meaning of the word organic is now in the hands of the government, which means it is subject to all the usual political and economic forces at play in Washington. The drive to keep organic food cheap will bring pressure to further weaken the regulations, and some of K Street's most skillful and influential lobbyists will soon be on the case. A couple of years ago, a chicken producer in Georgia named Fieldale Farms induced its congressman to slip a helpful provision into an Agriculture Department appropriations bill that would allow organic chicken farmers to substitute conventional chicken feed when the price of organic feed exceeded a certain level. Well, that certainly makes life easier for a chicken producer, especially when the price of organic corn is up around $8 a bushel (compared to less than $2 for conventional feed). But in what sense would a chicken fed on conventional feed still be organic? In no sense except the Orwellian one: because the government says it is. An outcry from consumers and wiser organic producers (who saw their precious label losing credibility) put a halt to Fieldale's plans, and the legislation was quickly repealed.

The moral of the Fieldale story is that unless consumers and well-meaning producers remain vigilant, the drive to make organic foods nearly as cheap as conventional foods threatens to hollow out the word and kill the gold-egg-laying organic goose. Let's hope Wal-Mart understands that the marketing power of the word organic—a power that flows directly from consumers' uneasiness about the conventional food chain—is a little like the health of a chicken living in close confinement with 20,000 other chickens in an organic CAFO, munching organic corn: fragile.

EVALUATING THE AUTHOR'S ARGUMENTS:

Pollan says that conventionally produced, cheap food actually has many hidden costs that in the end make it more expensive than organic food. What do you think he means by this? Flesh out a few ways in which conventional food might have hidden costs, and whether you think organic food should be sold in chain stores.

Organic Food in Chain Stores Offers Some Advantages

Ann Cooper and Kate Adamick

> *"When Wal-Mart adds low-priced organic produce to the shelves of its 3,400 stores ... chemical-free food will instantly be within the reach of tens of millions of individuals."*

Ann Cooper and Kate Adamick argue in the following viewpoint that industrially produced organic food has both positive and negative aspects. They explain that some things about industrial organic food are troubling, such as the long distances it travels and the fact that it is increasingly being offered in processed, junk food forms. But, they point out that when chain stores carry organic products, chemical-free food becomes available to millions of Americans who may not otherwise have access to it. They conclude that the government should take a more active role in ensuring the health and safety of the food supply. In addition, consumers should consider the hidden costs to the environment and society when considering purchases of mass-produced food, whether organic or not.

Ann Cooper and Kate Adamick, "An Organic Foods Dilemma: They're Mass-Produced by Agribiz but Better than Eating Poisons," *San Francisco Chronicle,* August 6, 2006. Reproduced by permission of the authors.

Cooper is director of nutrition services for the Berkeley Unified School District. Adamick is a food systems consultant in New York specializing in school food reform.

AS YOU READ, CONSIDER THE FOLLOWING QUESTIONS:
1. According to the authors, how does the amount Americans spend per capita on food compare with that of citizens of other industrialized countries?
2. What do the authors predict will happen should McDonald's switch to organic ingredients?
3. Name at least one "disquieting issue" the authors raise about industrial organic food.

"Industrial organics." The mere mention of the recently coined, aptly turned phrase describing mass-produced organic foods grown on giant industrial farms and sold in superstores such as Wal-Mart, Whole Foods and Safeway, can cause our palms to sweat.

Industrial Organics Pose a Difficult Dilemma

As food systems consultants and school food reform advocates, we regularly take a firm stand on a wide range of controversial food issues. So what is it about industrial organics that kicks our nervous systems into high gear? Is it that we so strongly believe that industrial organics constitute an incongruity so dangerous as to destroy any remaining prospect of developing a truly sustainable agriculture system? Or, is it because we fervently believe industrial organics are the long-awaited savior—almighty capitalism's answer to eradicating pesticides, hormones and antibiotics from our food supply?

The answer, we hesitate to admit, is neither. In fact, it is precisely because we are firmly entrenched in neither camp that, when confronted head-on with the issue, our bodies respond with auto reflex symptoms typical of the fight-or-flight syndrome. The reasons for our inability to arrive at a definitive conclusion are as complex as the evolution of the food system itself.

Big Brands Go Organic

Seeking to capitalize on the popularity of organics, some of the largest food companies in the world have created organic brands. Supporters say "industrial organics" put chemical-free food in the hands of more people.

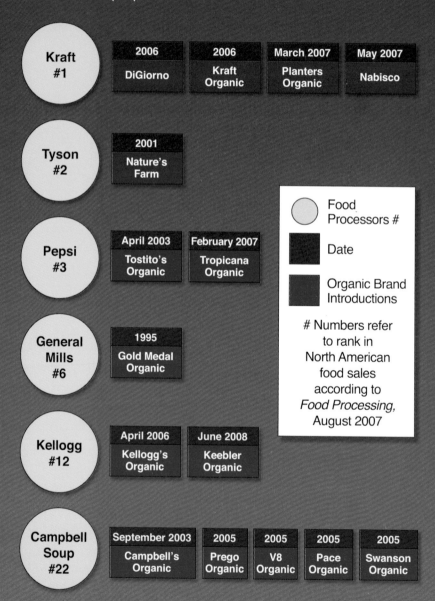

Kraft #1

2006	2006	March 2007	May 2007
DiGiorno	Kraft Organic	Planters Organic	Nabisco

Tyson #2

2001
Nature's Farm

Pepsi #3

April 2003	February 2007
Tostito's Organic	Tropicana Organic

General Mills #6

1995
Gold Medal Organic

Kellogg #12

April 2006	June 2008
Kellogg's Organic	Keebler Organic

Campbell Soup #22

September 2003	2005	2005	2005	2005
Campbell's Organic	Prego Organic	V8 Organic	Pace Organic	Swanson Organic

Legend:
- ○ Food Processors #
- ■ Date
- ■ Organic Brand Introductions

Numbers refer to rank in North American food sales according to *Food Processing*, August 2007

Taken from: Phil Howard, assistant professor, Dept. of Community, Agriculture, Recreation and Resource Studies Michigan State University, January 2008.

Held Captive by Conventional Foods

In recent decades, the rise of agribusiness—which was supported, if not actually created, by the U.S. Department of Agriculture—has given birth to food production and processing systems that promised cheap food and the eradication of hunger in America. Our modern food system, which is revered as the epitome of economic and production efficiency, generates meals in mass quantities with minimal labor, kitchen equipment and production time. As a result, Americans spend a smaller percentage of their per capita income on food than do the citizens of any other industrialized nation in the world.

Highly processed products, now conveniently located in nearly every grocery store in the United States, are readily available to anyone and everyone with enough cash, credit or food stamps to pay for them. Moreover, one would be hard pressed to turn the pages of a magazine or watch an hour of television without colliding with a multibillion-dollar annual marketing effort skillfully designed to convince us that such products are not only desirable but an essential part of a successful and happy life. Thus, most average Americans are, in essence, held captive by an industrialized food system destined—if not designed—to make them sick.

FAST FACT

More than 200 million Americans shop at Wal-Mart each year. It is argued that offering organic food to so many Americans can help improve nutrition in the United States.

One need only examine the paradox of obesity among the poor to understand the tragic truth that, rather than eradicating hunger with a steady supply of affordable and nutritious food, our current food system has helped create a country in which most of its citizens may be well-fed but few are fed well.

Making Chemical-Free Food Available to Everyone

It is precisely this fact that leads so many to enthusiastically endorse industrial organics, which encompass foods ranging from carrots to strawberry to wheat.

When Wal-Mart adds low-priced organic produce to the shelves of its 3,400 stores across middle and rural America, chemical-free food

The author argues that agribusiness lobbies the USDA to continually weaken the definition of what is "certified organic."

will instantly be within the reach of tens of millions of individuals currently without access to them. And once McDonald's begins serving organic beef patties, lettuce, cheese, pickles and onions on sesame seed buns made with organic wheat, conventionally grown versions of those products will become relics destined for the Smithsonian's collection.

How, then, can anyone argue that the ready accessibility of organic products is not cause for celebration? Isn't this exactly what those of us who preach the virtues of focusing on food quality, rather than simply on food quantity, have long been awaiting?

Industrial Organics Has Its Share of Problems

Our enthusiasm is tempered by the regrettable reality that industrial organics present a host of other disquieting issues.

Even organic products, when shipped cross-country and overseas, not only render moot the concepts of "seasonal" and "local," but exhaust our precious fuel supplies and emit steady streams of pollutants into our air and water.

Furthermore, the arrival of such anomalies as organic high fructose corn syrup and organic cookies on our grocery store shelves only mirrors the worst attributes of the conventional food system. And while attempting to convince us that higher demand for organics will create economies of scale that will result in lower production costs, the pressure to produce cheap organics already has agribusiness lobbying the USDA to allow more and more crop-enhancing chemicals within the ever-weakening definition of "certified organic." And if the promised economies of scale ever reach their predicted potential, still more family farmers will be driven off their land and into the employ of corporate mega-farms, trading their fiercely independent heritage for the hope of a steady paycheck.

Our government has largely turned its back on the health and well-being of both its citizens and the environment by relinquishing oversight of our food supply to corporate giants. Thus, corporate conglomerates will likely view industrial organics as the latest big money-making trend and do whatever it takes to keep consumers' attention blindly focused on their low prices, rather than on their high costs.

Until Americans are willing to pay a higher price for a food supply that is healthy for both us and our planet, we must—for better or worse—continue to chew on the moral dilemma that is industrial organics.

EVALUATING THE AUTHORS' ARGUMENTS:

The authors classify industrial organics as a "moral dilemma." In two or three sentences, explain what you think they mean by this. Then, write one or two sentences on how you think each of the other authors represented in this chapter would respond.

Facts About Organic Food and Farming

Editor's note: These facts can be used in reports to make important points or claims.

The U.S. Department of Agriculture first started placing an organic seal on food on October 21, 2002.

More than 30 percent of the global demand for organic food stems from the United States, according to *Nutrition Business Journal.*

Organic foods are particularly popular in California, New York, New Jersey, Wisconsin, Minnesota, Virginia, and Pennsylvania.

Internationally, organic foods are popular in Canada, Mexico, Austria, Denmark, Finland, France, Germany, Italy, the Netherlands, Spain, Sweden, Switzerland, UK, Hungary, Poland, Australia, New Zealand, China, India, Japan, Malaysia, Singapore, Thailand, Turkey, Argentina, Brazil, Chile, and South Africa.

Organic products are not limited to food. Many health stores sell lines of organic cosmetics, body products, shampoo and conditioners, clothing, and linens.

As per the Organic Foods Production Act, organic agriculture must use materials and practices that enhance the ecological balance of natural systems and that integrate the parts of the farming system into an ecological whole. Organic agriculture practices cannot ensure that products are completely free of residues, but methods are used to minimize pollution from air, soil, and water.

According to the Organic Consumers Association, it takes five years to convert soil that had been used in conventional farming to organic.

The Growth of the Organic Industry

According to the Organic Trade Association, in 2006:

- The U.S. organic industry grew 21 percent and accounted for $17.7 billion in consumer sales.
- Nonfood organic products (personal care products, nutritional supplements, household cleaners, flowers, pet food, and clothing, bedding, and other products from organic fibers such as flax, wool, and cotton) grew 26 percent and accounted for $938 million in U.S. sales.
- Organic foods and beverages accounted for $16.7 million in consumer sales.
- The fastest-growing food categories and their rates of growth over the previous year were:
  - organic meat (29 percent)
  - organic dairy products (25 percent)
  - organic fruits and vegetables (24 percent)
- The fastest-growing nonfood categories were:
  - organic pet food (36.7 percent)
  - household products/cleaners (31.6 percent)
  - fiber linens and clothing (26.9 percent)
- Mass-market grocery stores accounted for 38 percent of organic food sales.
- Large natural food chains, along with small natural food chains or independent natural groceries and health food stores, represented about 44 percent of organic food sales.
- About 2 percent of organic food is sold through farmers' markets.

The Price of Organic Food

In 2008 the *New York Times* surveyed organic products and conventional products in four grocery stores around the country. They found that organic food typically costs 20 percent to 100 percent more than its conventional counterpart:

	Regular	Organic
Bread:	$1.19–$3.79	$3.19–$4.55
Eggs:	$1.34–$3.59	$3.99–$6.39
Milk:	$1.99–$2.99	$3.29–$4.99
Spaghetti:	$1.09–$2.39	$1.99–$3.59
Yogurt:	$0.89–$1.99	$0.99–$3.29

American Opinions About Organic Food

A 2007 Harris poll revealed the following opinions Americans hold about organic food:

- Only 7 percent of all adults report buying organic food "all or most of the time."
- 31 percent say they buy it occasionally.
- 33 percent say they rarely buy organic food.
- 26 percent say they never buy organic food.
- Some segments of the population are more likely to buy organic foods regularly:
    - college graduates (11 percent)
    - liberals (11 percent)
    - Westerners (10 percent)
    - 18–30-year-olds (10 percent)
    - 31–42-year-olds (9 percent)
- 95 percent of Americans believe organic food is more expensive than conventional foods.
- 84 percent believe organic food is grown with fewer pesticides.
- 79 percent believe that organic food is safer for the environment.
- 76 percent believe that organic food is healthier.
- 86 percent of people who buy organic food frequently also think it tastes better.
- 39 percent of all adults think organic food tastes better.
- 36 percent of Americans believe that "organic food is much better for you" and that "the extra expense is worth it to have better food."
- 29 percent of Americans believe organic food is "a waste of money as it is no better for you than conventional foods."
- 36 percent are not sure.

According to a November 2008 poll taken by *Consumer Reports:*

- 93 percent of consumers said that fish labeled organic should be fed 100 percent organic feed (this was in response to a 2008 recommendation from the National Organic Standards Board that said organic fish could be fed nonorganic fishmeal).
- 90 percent of consumers said that organic fish farms should be required to recover all waste so it cannot pollute the environment.
- 57 percent of consumers said they are concerned about ocean pollution caused by fish farms advertised as organic.

- 93 percent of consumers polled said that dairies that produce milk and milk products without artificial growth hormones should be allowed to label their products as being free of these hormones.
- 70 percent of consumers polled are concerned about dairy cows being given synthetic growth hormones.
- 95 percent of consumers polled agree that food products made from genetically engineered animals should be labeled as such.
- 94 percent of consumers polled agree that meat and dairy products from cloned animals should be labeled as such.
- 58 percent of consumers polled are concerned about eating meat or milk products from cloned or genetically engineered animals.

Organizations to Contact

The editor has compiled the following list of organizations concerned with the issues debated in this book. The descriptions are derived from materials provided by the organizations. All have publications or information available for interested readers. The list was compiled on the date of publication of the present volume; the information provided here may change. Be aware that many organizations take several weeks or longer to respond to queries, so allow as much time as possible.

American Council on Science and Health (ACSH)
1995 Broadway, 2nd Flr.
New York, NY 10023-5860
(212) 362-7044
e-mail: acsh@acsh.org
Web site: www.acsh.org

ACSH provides consumers with scientific evaluations of food and the environment, pointing out both health hazards and benefits. It participates in a variety of government and media events, from congressional hearings to popular magazines.

Campaign for Food Safety (CFS)
6101 Cliff Estate Rd.
Little Marais, MN 55614
(218) 226-4164
Web site: www.purefood.org

The Campaign for Food Safety promotes the growth of organic and sustainable agriculture practices. CFS activist strategies include education, boycotts, grassroots lobbying, litigation, networking, direct action protests, and media events.

Cato Institute
1000 Massachusetts Ave. NW
Washington, DC 20001-5403

(202) 842-0200
fax: (202) 842-3490
e-mail: cato@cato.org
Web site: www.cato.org

The institute is a libertarian public policy research foundation dedicated to limiting the role of government and protecting individual liberties. It asserts that the concern over the possible health risks of pesticide use in agriculture is overstated. The institute publishes the quarterly *Cato Journal*, the bimonthly *Cato Policy Report*, and numerous books and commentaries.

Center for Science in the Public Interest (CSPI)
1875 Connecticut Ave. NW, Ste. 300
Washington, DC 20009
(202) 332-9110
e-mail: cspi@cspinet.org
Web site: www.cspinet.org

The CSPI is a nonprofit education and advocacy organization committed to improving the safety and nutritional quality of the U.S. food supply.

Cornucopia Institute
PO Box 126
Cornucopia, WI 54827
(608) 625-2042
e-mail: cultivate@cornucopia.org
Web site: www.cornucopia.org

The Cornucopia Institute's mission is to promote economic justice for family farming. It supports educational activities that spread the ecological principles and economic wisdom that underlie sustainable and organic agriculture. Through research and investigations on agricultural issues, the Cornucopia Institute provides information to consumers, family farmers, and the media about organic food and farming.

Environmental Protection Agency (EPA)
Ariel Rios Bldg.
1200 Pennsylvania Ave. NW
Washington, DC 20460

(202) 272-0167
Web site: www.epa.gov

The EPA is a government agency that regulates pesticides under two major federal statutes. It establishes maximum legally permissible levels for pesticide residues in food, registers pesticides for use in the United States, and prescribes labeling and other regulatory requirements to prevent unreasonable adverse effects on health or the environment.

Food and Drug Administration (FDA)
10903 New Hampshire Ave.
Silver Spring, MD 20903
(888) 463-6332
Web site: www.fda.gov

The FDA is a public health agency charged with protecting American consumers by enforcing the Federal Food, Drug, and Cosmetic Act and several related public health laws. To carry out this mandate of consumer protection, FDA has investigators and inspectors cover the country's almost ninety-five thousand FDA-regulated businesses. Its publications include government documents, reports, fact sheets, and press announcements.

Food First Institute for Food and Development Policy
398 Sixtieth St.
Oakland, CA 94618
(510) 654-4400
Web site: www.foodfirst.org

Food First, cofounded by Frances Moore Lappé, the author of *Diet for a Small Planet*, promotes sustainable agriculture. Its current projects include the Cuban Organic Agriculture Exchange Program and Californians for Pesticide Reform.

Food Safety Consortium (FSC)
110 Agriculture Bldg.
University of Arkansas
Fayetteville, AR 72701
(501) 575-5647
Web site: www.uark.edu/depts/fsc

Congress established the Food Safety Consortium, consisting of researchers from the University of Arkansas, Iowa State University, and Kansas State University, in 1988 through a special Cooperative State Research Service grant. The FSC conducts extensive investigation into all areas of poultry, beef, and pork production.

Friends of the Earth (FoE)
1717 Massachusetts Ave. NW, Ste. 600
Washington, DC 20036
(202) 783-7400
e-mail: foe@foe.org
Web site: www.foe.org

Friends of the Earth monitors legislation and regulations that affect the environment. Its Safer Food, Safer Farms Campaign speaks out against what it perceives as the negative impact biotechnology can have on farming, food production, genetic resources, and the environment.

Organic Agriculture and Products Education Institute (Organic Institute)
PO Box 547
Greenfield, MA 01302
Web site: www.theorganicinstitute.org

The Organic Institute was created by members of the Organic Trade Association. Its mission is to educate about the attributes, benefits, and practices of organic agriculture and products today for better environmental and personal health tomorrow. Its Web site offers a downloadable guide for students who want to bring organic dining to their school or college campus.

Organic Trade Association (OTA)
PO Box 547
Greenfield, MA 01302
(413) 774-7511
Web site: www.ota.com

The Organic Trade Association is a membership-based business association that focuses on the organic business community in North America.

OTA's mission is to promote and protect the growth of organic trade to benefit the environment, farmers, the public, and the economy.

Rodale Institute
611 Siegfriedale Rd.
Kutztown, PA 19530-9320
(610) 683-1400
e-mail: info@rodaleinst.org
Web site: www.rodaleinstitute.org

The Rodale Institute was founded in 1947 by organic pioneer J.I. Rodale. The institute employs soil scientists and a cooperating network of researchers who document how organic farming techniques offer the best solution to global warming and famine. Its Web site offers information on the longest-running U.S. study comparing organic and conventional farming techniques, which is the basis for Rodale's practical training to thousands of farmers in Africa, Asia, and the Americas.

U.S. Department of Agriculture (USDA)
1400 Independence Ave. SW
Washington, DC 20250
Web site: www.usda.gov

This government organization is charged with regulating the standards for any farm, wild crop harvesting, or handling operation that wants to sell an agricultural product as organically produced. The USDA has set requirements for the importing and exporting of organic products. More information about this process is available on its Web site, as are numerous fact sheets and publications about the state of food in America.

For Further Reading

Books

Avery, Alex. *The Truth About Organic Foods.* St. Louis, MO: Henderson Communications, 2006.

Burke, Cindy. *To Buy or Not to Buy Organic: What You Need to Know to Choose the Healthiest, Safest, Most Earth-Friendly Food.* Cambridge, MA: Da Capo, 2007.

Fromartz, Samuel. *Organic, Inc.: Natural Foods and How They Grew.* Fort Washington, PA: Harvest, 2007.

Gilman, Jeff. *The Truth About Organic Gardening: Benefits, Drawbacks, and the Bottom Line.* Portland, OR: Timber, 2008.

Nestle, Marion. *What to Eat.* New York: North Point, 2007.

Pollan, Michael. *In Defense of Food: An Eater's Manifesto.* New York: Penguin, 2009.

Ronald, Pamela C., and R.W. Adamchak. *Tomorrow's Table: Organic Farming, Genetics, and the Future of Food.* New York: Oxford University Press, 2008.

Periodicals

Allen, Kimberly Jordan. "Edible History: Discovering the Benefits of Heirloom Fruits and Vegetables," *E,* May/June 2005.

Callaway, Ewen. "Food Miles Don't Feed Climate Change—Meat Does," *New Scientist,* April 18, 2008. www.newscientist.com/article/dn13741.

Cloud, John. "Eating Better than Organic," *Time,* March 2, 2007. www.time.com/time/magazine/article/0,9171,1595245,00.html.

Cummins, Ronnie. "The Food, Climate, and Energy Crisis: From Panic to Organic," CommonDreams.org, June 13, 2008. www.commondreams.org/archive/2008/06/13/9601.

Foreman, Judy. "Weighing the Value of Organic Foods," *Los Angeles Times,* December 1, 2008. http://articles.latimes.com/2008/dec/01/health/he-organic1.

Gogoi, Pallavi. "Are Wal-Mart's 'Organics' Organic?" *Business Week*, January 18, 2007. www.businessweek.com/bwdaily/dnflash/content/jan2007/db20070117_887392.htm.

Goodman, Jim. "Organic Farming, Promise in the Face of Global Warming," Common Dreams.org, February 26, 2009. www.commondreams.org/view/2009/02/26-0.

Hastings, Max. "Overpriced and Over-hyped, Don't Believe All You Read About Organic Food," *Daily Mail* (London), October 30, 2007. www.dailymail.co.uk/debate/columnists/article-490609/Overpriced-hyped-dont-believe-read-organic-food.html.

LaSalle, Tim J., and Paul Hepperly, "Regenerative Organic Farming: A Solution to Global Warming," Rodale Institute, July 2008. www.rodaleinstitute.org/files/Rodale_Research_Paper-07_30_08.pdf.

Leahy, Stephen. "Peak Soil: The Silent Global Crisis," *Earth Island Journal*, vol. 23, no. 1, Spring 2008.

Leonard, Andrew. "Organic Farming—Not Sustainable?" Salon.com, February 21, 2007. www.salon.com/tech/htww/2007/02/21/organic_farming.

Mark, Jason. "Neat Freaks: How Food Safety Rules Are Threatening Environmentally Friendly Farming Practices," *Earth Island Journal*, vol. 23, no. 1, Spring 2008.

McKie, Robin. "How the Myth of Food Miles Hurts the Planet," *Guardian* (Manchester, UK), March 23, 2008. www.guardian.co.uk/environment/2008/mar/23/food.ethicalliving.

Miller, John J. "The Organic Myth: A Food Movement Makes a Pest of Itself," *National Review*, vol. 56, no. 2, February 9, 2004.

Milmo, Cahal. "Organic Farming 'No Better for the Environment,'" *Independent* (London), February 19, 2007. www.independent.co.uk/environment/green-living/organic-farming-no-better-for-the-environment-436949.html.

Niles, Meredith. "Food Security and Global Warming: Monsanto Versus Organic," *Grist*, January 14, 2009. http://gristmill.grist.org/story/2009/1/14/23742/0777.

Parker-Pope, Tara. "For Three Years, Every Bite Organic," *New York Times*, December 2, 2008. www.nytimes.com/2008/12/02/health/02well.html?_r=1&8dpc.

Philpott, Tom. "Up Against the Wal-Mart: Big Buyers Make Organic Farmers Feel Smaller than Ever," *Grist*, August 23, 2006. www.grist .org/comments/food/2006/08/23/buyers/.

———. "What I Saw at the Summit: Thoughts from the Big Organic Confab in Boulder," *Grist*, July 1, 2008. http://gristmill.grist.org/ story/2008/6/30/21327/8515.

Rich, Deborah K. "Organic Fruits and Vegetables Work Harder for Their Nutrients: Produce Has Been Losing Vitamins and Minerals over the Past Half-Century," *San Francisco Chronicle*, March 25, 2006. www .sfgate.com/cgi-bin/article.cgi?f=/c/a/2006/03/25/HOG3BHSDPG1 .DTL.

Weis, Rice. "Can Food from Cloned Animals Be Called Organic?" *Washington Post*, January 29, 2008. www.washingtonpost.com/ wp-dyn/content/article/2007/01/28/AR2007012800862.html.

Whitney, Jake. "Organic Erosion: Will the Term Organic Still Mean Anything When It's Adopted Whole Hog by Behemoths Such as Wal-Mart?" *San Francisco Chronicle*, January 28, 2007. https://ofrf.org/ pressroom/organic_news_clips/070128_sfchronicle_organicerosion .pdf.

Web Sites

National Organic Program (NOP) (www.ams.usda.gov/nop). This Web site, maintained by the U.S. Department of Agriculture, develops, implements, and administers national production, handling, and labeling standards for organic agricultural products. The NOP also accredits the certifying agents (foreign and domestic) who inspect organic production and handling operations to certify that they meet USDA standards.

Organic Consumers Organization (OCO) (www.organicconsumers .org). This Web site promotes the views and interests of the nation's estimated 50 million organic consumers. The OCA deals with crucial issues of food safety, industrial agriculture, genetic engineering, children's health, corporate accountability, fair trade, environmental sustainability, and other topics.

Organic: It's Worth It (www.organicitsworthit.com). This Web site shows kids, adults, teachers, and parents why choosing organic foods makes a difference for families, health, the environment, and the community.

Organic.org (www.organic.org). Contains links to news, product reviews, other food, and information regarding organic food and farming products.

World Wide Opportunities on Organic Farms (WWOOF) (www. wwoof.org). WWOOF is an international movement that helps people share more sustainable ways of living. It links people who want to volunteer on organic farms with people who are looking for volunteer help. In return for volunteer help, WWOOF hosts offer food, accommodations, and opportunities to learn about organic lifestyles.

Index

Picture Credits

Daniel Acker/Bloomberg News/Landov, 79
AP Images, 8, 36, 49, 92, 94, 97, 105, 111, 118
Gaetan Bally/Keystone/Landov, 53
Amit Bhargava/Bloomberg News/Landov, 83
Matt Cardy/Getty Images, 28
Tim Graham/Getty Images, 23
© Nick Gregory/Alamy, 41
© LWA-Dann Tardif/Corbis, 15
Enrique Marcarian/Reuters/Landov, 69
Jessica Rinaldi/Reuters/Landov, 58
SciMAT/Photo Researchers, Inc., 62
© Peter Titmuss/Alamy, 11
Steve Zmina, 16, 21, 35, 42, 56, 64, 71, 76, 85, 90, 104, 116